GW00598140

With love to Nicholas and Saoirse

STORIES OF HOPE

VALERIE BOWE

LONDUBH BOOKS

First published in 2010 by Londubh Books

18 Casimir Avenue, Harold's Cross, Dublin 6w

www. londubh. ie

3 5 4 2

Cover by red rattle design; origination by Londubh Books

Printed in Ireland by ColourBooks, Baldoyle Industrial Estate, Dublin 13

ISBN: 978-1-907535-17-8

Part of the proceeds of this book will go to the Kitty Whittle Fund, which provides education bursaries for lone parents.

Acknowledgements

I am deeply appreciative of Jo O'Donoghue of Londubh Books who approached me with the idea for this book and invited me to compile it. It was an invitation I was only too delighted to accept.

I am also very grateful to all the organisations and individuals who facilitated me in gathering the stories in this book: Social Anxiety Ireland, the Family Support Network, Supporting People Affected by Mental Ill-Health (SHINE), the Star Project, Henrietta Adult and Community Association (HACE), Lourdes Youth and Community Services (LYCS), Down Syndrome Ireland, Irish Seal Sanctuary, Open Heart House, the Carers' Association, Tullamore, the Irish Motor Neurone Disease Association, the Asthma Society of Ireland, the Irish Countrywomen's Association, Bodywhys, the Jack & Jill Foundation, the Irish Kidney Association, Red Cross Ireland, Spina Bifida Hydrocephalus Ireland, AMEN; and to Rachael Dempsey, Shelia Smith, Molly O'Duffy, Helena McNeill and Mickey McCormick.

Thanks to all the contributors who so generously contributed to the book, some of whom have used their own names and others who wish to remain anonymous.

Thanks also to my late parents: my mother whose beautiful warm smile could beam you up and my father whose great sense of occasion and style tinged the world with an aura of excitement.

Thank you all.

INTRODUCTION

I have worked in the voluntary/community sector for quite a number of years now. Many people have chatted to me about their lives and some would have confided in me. I have never failed to be struck by life's quiet heroes: people who, without any fanfare, have overcome great difficulties despite all the odds against them. I couldn't say that there is any one thing that I have learned that I could wrap up and impart to you here. However, life has taught me that support and awareness are of paramount importance and that acceptance brings us all to a place of serenity. I also know that the Beatles hit the high note when they sang, 'Love is all there is.'

In addition, I have learned that telling our stories is a remarkable first step and from this comes a ripple effect. Maybe when we tell our story our life is acknowledged both to ourselves and to the listener. It is shared; it is witnessed, so to speak. When this process is supportive, only good can happen.

Some contributors in this book have shared their

life stories with us. For many contributors it has been a question of survival – and survival has its own congratulations. Others have shared a significant event in their lives, an event they have navigated, keeping the spark of hope alive until the road turned for them.

One thing I learned from compiling *Stories of Hope* is that hope can sometimes ravage us. I have spoken to people who had to give up hope. They said it was killing them. They were hoping for a particular outcome and when it wasn't happening, they had to surrender and accept the situation. Their resistance left them and a peace emerged. They gave up the fight – but they didn't give up. Even when all hope is gone – it seems there is something else – trust.

I hope you like the stories in this book. The contributors have been admirable in their openness and I know that you, the readers, will see this your-selves and applaud them for it. If you would like to get in touch with me my email address is valentinebowe@gmail.com.

Please note: where Christian names only are given, some of these have been changed for reasons of confidentiality.

Valerie Bowe, October 2010

Contents

Stories
of Hope

The darkest hour is just before the dawn.

GET OFF MY CAR

Kay, Dublin

When I moved into my new council house I had a little Fiat car. Sometimes the children would gather round the car when I drove in, mostly out of curiosity about the child in the car, my daughter, whom they wanted to get to know. But one day I looked out my window and one of the children, a young boy, was up dancing on the car roof. When he saw me he looked defiant. I told him to get down off the roof and said I was going to tell his mother. He stayed up on the roof. I persisted and after a few minutes he got down.

By this time I had got to know a few of the neighbours. I was cautioned not to approach this family as they were 'trouble'. People almost trembled at the thought of my going to this boy's mother. I was beginning to feel scared myself but I thought, 'If I don't do something this young boy will walk all over me and my car!'

If everyone was afraid of the family, I needed to be very careful. I thought about how I would approach it. I would call to the door and use myself as an example, my own situation, and work it from there. So when the mother opened the door, I didn't get to the point straight away. I talked around it. I said I didn't want to bring trouble to her door but that if she had any difficulty with my child I would welcome her coming to me as that would give me an opportunity to correct my daughter. I said to her I just needed to let her know that her boy was on the roof of my car and asked if she would tell him not to do it again. I emphasised that I was sorry to have to come to her door.

At this stage, I was pretty nervous but she seemed fine and was prepared to listen. She didn't get defensive. She apologised for her son. 'I won't be hitting him,' she said.

'Oh no, no, I wouldn't want you to do that,' I said, 'just if you could have a talk with him.'

'I'll be grounding him,' she informed me. 'He'll be grounded for a week.'

She then told me why she disciplined her boy by grounding. 'I don't hit him any more. I used to have to be torn off him until I went to Barnardos.'

'I'm Leaving...'

Anonymous

It was only June and 1999 had not been a good year so far. My mum had died, my dad was diagnosed with dementia and I would have to go into hospital for an operation in July.

Then one Saturday night, when I thought things could not really get any worse, we were in the middle of dinner and my husband says, as casually as he'd ask me to pass him the salt, 'I've met someone else. I'm leaving.'

And he did. Just like that. Packed a bag and took off into the sunset with a young one.

We were married in the early 1970s when it was the norm for a young married woman to give up her job and become a full-time mother as soon as her first child was born. This is what I did.

So there I was twenty-five years later. No skills that were relevant any more; no income except the varying amounts of cash that he would send periodically, via my fourteen-year-old, instructing him to, 'Give that to your mother.' What could I do?

Misery…hurt…despair…panic. They all came one after the other, riding along on great waves of hopelessness and self-pity.

I had started a four-year degree course the previous September. How was I going to finish it now? It was my only hope of a decent job. I was doomed to shelf-stacking, if indeed I could get a job doing that.

On the positive side, legally we were able to stay in the house, which was the family home, until my youngest finished school. My husband would continue paying the mortgage until then and at that point we would have to sell it and divide the money from the sale.

After the operation I really needed a break. I asked a friend if she would come away with me for a week. 'Somewhere cheap but warm,' I said.

She looked at me and said, 'Get into a plane with you? You must be joking. With your luck it'd probably crash before it took off!'

I looked at her and we burst out laughing. We laughed till we cried. It was the best thing that had happened to me all summer.

Laughter is such an amazing medicine. I knew there and then that I was going to get through this and come out the other end a stronger and better person

I returned to my course in September and did so many part-time jobs in the evenings and at weekends to support us that I had to keep a timetable to see where I was supposed to be and when!

Three years later I'd made it and I made some great new friends along the way.

The inevitable court case and divorce finally happened. I was dreading selling the house but leaving it and getting my own place were the final breaks with the past that I needed.

I now have a job I love and a home of my own. I am a stronger happier person than I ever imagined I could be and I know that we all have it in us to achieve anything, no matter what.

THE IBIZA PARTY

Fergal McLoughlin, Dublin

Twenty-three years ago I had cancer. On Good Friday 1987, they opened up my back in St Vincent's Hospital to try to find out what was wrong. For the previous six months I had suffered excruciating pain at the base of my spine. Assessments varied from arthritis to a slipped disc. Drugged out of my mind with morphine, I collapsed on the stairs at home and split my head on a glass partition. I was rushed to hospital and lay in agony until they operated on that fateful Good Friday.

Three weeks and many pathology tests later, the doctor told me the news. Non-Hodgkins lymphoma. Cancer. It was a strange feeling. At least they knew what was causing the problem. But surely cancer meant death?

'How long have I got?' I asked.

'Difficult to say,' he said.' We'll put you on a full course of treatment.'

His manner was sympathetic but the atmosphere

was funereal. My wife Judy came in. We held each other silently in a mixture of love and dread. Later she told me she had known the bad news for the previous three weeks. It gave me great strength to know that she loved me so dearly that she had protected me from the shock in my post-operative state.

Prior to the doctor's visit that day I had been reading Daniel Defoe's book *Robinson Crusoe*. I revisited what he had written: 'These reflections made me sensible to the Goodness of Providence to me, and very thankful for my present condition, with all its hardships and misfortunes; and this part I cannot but recommend to the reflection of those who are apt in their misery to say: is any affliction like mine?'

I lay awake in the darkness of the ward that night. In the midst of my fear and loneliness, I acknowledged two things: I was blessed with a beautiful wife and two lovely children; and I believed totally that I could be cured. The latter was a strong feeling but there was a nagging doubt. What could I do? It was decided that I would have radiotherapy followed by chemotherapy. The doctors and nurses were superb but I felt there was something I should be doing, rather than leaving it all to them. But what?

One day as I lay in bed I read an article by a woman called Penny Brohn. She had cured herself of breast cancer, based on an extraordinary belief in the power of the body to heal itself – a belief in body, mind and spirit. Hope.

I got her book, *Gentle Giants*, and devoured its contents. I read that she had founded the Bristol Cancer Help Centre which practised what she had discovered on her personal journey: that recovery was 'a process, a whole series of healings, lots of events all strung together.' I read about diet, counselling, healing, relaxation, meditation, visualisation.

I realised my life was a mess. I worried unduly. I was stressed about my job. I drank too much. I resolved to delve into this Bristol stuff – at worst it would do no harm, at best it would boost what the medics were doing. Something I could do myself. Hope. During chemotherapy, with the drip in my arm, I practised visualisation. I pictured myself well and healthy. I pictured the tumour diminishing in size, my blood cells returning to normal.

When I left hospital I spent a week in the Bristol Cancer Help Centre. I met the inspirational Penny Brohn and I experienced with a small group of fellow patients what we could do for ourselves. I came away more convinced than ever that it was possible to be fully cured. I changed my diet. I practiced meditation. I reconnected with the spiritual side of my life.

And so it came to pass. Two years later I was well on the road to recovery. I remembered an ambulance trip from St Vincent's to St Luke's Hospital for treatment.

The driver, a true Dub, said to me: 'Are you going to have an Ibiza party?'

I thought he was mad. 'What are you talking about?' I asked.

'An "I beat it" party – ya know – I beat it – the big C!'

How right he was. And ever since it has been an unending party – a thanksgiving for the gift of life, for the gift of health, for the power of hope and love.

A Day in January

Maria, County Dublin

My story is one of support and friendship. Without them I wouldn't be sitting down and writing this today.

The event that brought huge change into my life and that of my family took place in the month of January more than ten years ago. I remember my husband, then in what one would call 'the prime of life', bending over to kiss me goodbye before setting off from our County Dublin home for a meeting in Galway.

'Mind the roads,' he warned, knowing I'd be venturing out in the car later in the day. 'They look treacherous.' I just about managed a sleepy grunt of acknowledgement from beneath the duvet as I heard him close the bedroom door behind him.

It was late afternoon when I got the phone call. My husband had suffered a major stroke, the voice at the other end of the line told me, slumping over in his chair shortly after the meeting had started. He'd been taken to Regional Hospital in Galway.

After the first frantic journey to his bedside, accompanied by my two equally dazed teenage children, long weeks of to-ing and fro-ing between Dublin and Galway ensued. Eventually we managed to have him transferred to a hospital in Dublin and finally, after weeks of treatment, were able to take him home. After that the months and years of 'hope' kicked in, hope that I'd get back the husband I once knew and loved so well, that my children would get back the dad who idolised them and made them laugh so much. But one day I just had to face that I had to let go of the stranglehold I had on 'hope', had to set it free and accept that this was the way life was going to be, that there was no going back to that January morning when life had been good – which now seemed to be part of another world.

While I was blessed with the family and friends I had, and equally good neighbours, I felt I had burdened them enough with the constant relating of my troubles every time we met and that, perhaps, starting up with something fresh might be good for me. By chance I saw a notice in the local parish newsletter saying that a Guild of the ICA (Irish Countrywomen's Association) was being formed in our area. I went to the information night, expecting to find a handful of women there, to discover that there was standing room only in the school hall! Within weeks, the guild was up and running and I'd signed up for membership.

Over the first few months, I formed tentative friendships, which in time grew and blossomed. I discovered that behind many of the smiling, laughing faces of my fellow members were stories far more harrowing than mine – stories of young widowhood, of the loss of children, of marriages that sadly hadn't worked out, of battles with cancer not once, but twice! I admired these women immensely for being able to put their troubles aside for those few hours we spent together each week, participating fully in whatever the guild was doing, whether it be bowling, a trip to the theatre, or revelling in the wit of Senator David Norris when he came to talk to us about James Joyce. I realised how lucky I'd been to have had twenty-five good years of marriage before my troubles struck.

And so I began to count my blessings and draw strength from these wonderful women whose company I share each Wednesday night, now sacrosanct in my diary. Their support buoys me when, every so often, a wave of sadness hits. I hope I may have said or done some small thing that helped them too.

LINDA

Linda Hyland, Dublin

I was working in a takeaway and a guy from Eastern Europe who was working with me was getting texts from this girl. When he was texting her back he kept asking me how to spell things. For the first few days I was able to help him with easy things but then it was getting harder and harder. 'Why don't you know? You're Irish,' he said to me. 'Excuse me you, I left school at fourteen,' I said. I went home crying. I was thinking of leaving the job.

My boyfriend said to me, 'You can't be like this,' and he brought me down to Larkin Community College where I met Marie and Nuala. I was very nervous and was thinking of running out but they were real nice. I got a one-to-one tutor. After a while she went to have a baby and they put me in a class with three other girls. I did my FETAC Certificate, which is the equivalent of the Junior Certificate.

One night my boyfriend was receiving his

certificate for a course he did in Henrietta Adult and
Community Education (HACE) and I went with him.
I asked the coordinator if I could do the cookery
course there. During the course I was asked to help
out with the sale of work. Then I became a volunteer
on the front desk: I would answer the phone, sign
people in on attendance sheets and when it wasn't too
busy I could do my crochet.

One day the coordinator tricked me into going to
a meeting! She asked me if I would go along and find
out a little bit more about a new course that was going
on. I went to the wrong place – I was the only white
person in the room!

We all got chatting. The facilitator explained to
me that the course was called Women as Leaders and
that it would go on for a couple of years. For the first
year two groups would work separately – one group
of Irishwomen (that's where I was meant to go) and
another group of women from different countries,
cultures and religions. Then for the second year the
two groups would come together. I stayed that day
and we had a great time. The other women were
encouraging me to do the course and I was saying, 'I
can't spell and my confidence isn't great.'

I decided to do the course. We learned about
different cultures, about the conflict in Palestine,

about politics. That course changed my life. One tutor, Noreen, created the monster in me. She taught me how to say 'No'. I won't be roped into things any more. I am doing things I would never have done. I go away on my own now, I voice my opinions around politics. On the course we were always talking about childcare and health services for women. Before I wouldn't have been watching out for things like that but now I watch the *News* and *Frontline* and *Tonight with Vincent Browne.*

I then trained to be a literacy tutor. Everybody is different. Some people just want to be able to learn how to use an ATM machine, others want to learn how to text and some people have trouble with numbers. The person I was working with wanted to learn how to write a letter, what to say and how to start it and finish it. I still get panicky spelling.

One day I was out having a cup of coffee with the coordinator when she got a phone call. The sewing tutor was sick. She said to me, 'You used to work in a sewing factory. Will you take the sewing class tonight?' After a lot of persuasion I did it! I was later asked to do a crochet workshop for the HACE summer school and for the past two years I have been teaching crochet.

I can't believe it when I see my name on the top of

the class attendance sheet as 'Tutor'. I always said if I had confidence I'd be dangerous and I am!

'DON'T WORRY, DADDY...'

Dáithí, County Meath

On 16 November 2008 my daughter Louise was born in the Rotunda Hospital in Dublin. She was five weeks premature and weighed in at a little over five pounds. To her mother and me she was a little miracle. The story that was to unfold was one of sheer horror and then the ultimate of joys. Louise had come to us via the HARI (Human Assisted Reproduction Ireland) clinic in the Rotunda, as for medical reasons we had difficulties conceiving naturally.

I will never forget sitting in a room with a counsellor and Bridget while the counsellor explained what lay ahead. As she talked I found myself drifting off and a little voice saying, 'Don't worry, Daddy, I am on my way.' I came back into the room and felt a little silly for letting myself wander off during such an important discussion. But from that moment on I made a connection with my daughter that was to carry me through my darkest moments and help me to face my greatest fears. I embarked on a journey that day in the clinic that was to change my life.

The pregnancy was difficult at different stages. Bridget suffered several bad bleeds. At one point while she was on a break in Donegal she had a suspected miscarriage. It was horrendous for her as a doctor on call told her that the baby had died, when, in fact, the baby was fine, according to a doctor in Letterkenny hospital some hours later. I listened to Bridget telling me this story on the telephone, feeling utterly helpless. Despite this and other difficulties I always came back to that voice reassuring me. During walks with the dogs in the fields near our house I sensed my daughter laughing and playing. It was as if she was watching over me. She gave me strength in her own way, letting me know that I should trust, that all would be fine.

Bridget was taken into hospital six weeks before the baby was due. A week into her stay the surgeons performed a Caesarean section at short notice due to the dangerous position of Louise in the womb. I was beside Bridget as my daughter came into this world. She needed assistance to start breathing and I watched in agony, for what seemed an eternity, as the nurses held Louise upside down, assisting her to give her first cry. While Bridget was being stitched by the surgeon I had the joy of giving my new little girl her first feed. Words cannot describe how proud I felt. I was walking on clouds.

The following day Louise was in intensive care and we were informed that our seemingly healthy daughter had a serious bowel condition called NEC (necro-tising enterocolitis). We watched, utterly helpless, as our precious girl lay in an incubator hooked up to a myriad wires and monitors. We were informed that all that could be done was to watch and wait. On day four Louise was fighting for her life and we were told that she was being rushed to Temple Street hospital for an emergency operation. We got to hold her before she left in case it was to be our last time. I went out into the corridor and cried with sheer frustration. A father was meant to protect his children and I felt utterly helpless. Then I got a flashback to that day in the clinic and thought that my little girl had come too far not to make it now. I let hope fill every little part of me.

The rest of that day remains a blur. I rang a close friend who told me that an issue with the bowel was all about letting go. Bridget and I let go that day. We handed over all our fears and asked our little girl to do the same. While I waited in the family room with our parents for the hours of that operation I decided that if Louise were to make it I would not wrap her up in cotton wool for the rest of her life but would enjoy every moment of time with her and let go so she could be exactly who she needed to be in life. When the theatre nurse walked into that room I knew by her face before she even spoke that our baby had made it.

The months that followed were difficult at times but Louise eventually recovered fully. So many people prayed, lit candles, sent messages of good luck for Louise that the energy around her was fantastic. She was a conduit for so much love and hope.

Today she is twenty months old and so full of life it's amazing. Her mother is wonderful with her and I know she has endured her own journey to get where she is today.

As a father I look into my daughter's eyes and it's as if I can see right into her heart. I sometimes feel I will explode with love. She and my son Ciaran give me hope for the future, two children carrying unconditional love and a wonderful energy around them.

I Tried To Be a Better Girlfriend

Pauline Bergin, Dublin

At twenty-four, I fell in love. At first it was exciting and new. After six months, the jealousy started, I put it down to his insecurity and tried to be a 'better girlfriend'. It was subtle at first and before I knew what was happening, he had started to control me.

The first time he called me a 'slut', I looked around to see who he was talking to. It couldn't be me! But that was the first of many such occasions. It was the start of the abusive relationship in which I was to spend another four years.

I remember all too clearly feeling humiliated by the way he spoke to me, made me feel small. The scars of emotional abuse are very real and they run deep. In fact, emotional abuse can be just as damaging as physical abuse – sometimes even more so. Again I kept minimising what was going on, excusing his behaviour, trying to find ways to 'keep the peace'.

The first time he hit me was with a chair. We had

just moved into our first new home and he threw it at me. I could not believe what was happening; I was numb with shock and I remember feeling very trapped and alone. Of course a part of me knew this was wrong and that he was wrong but I stayed in denial. The abuse continued: psychological, verbal and physical, sometimes leaving me battered and bruised as well as broken-hearted.

The worst part was knowing that this was not the life I was destined for but I felt powerless to get out. I knew a part of me was slowly dying, the part that believed I deserved better, the part that needed to fight back: this had long since gone.

The emotional and psychological consequences of domestic abuse are severe. Emotionally abusive relationships can destroy your self-worth, lead to anxiety and depression and make you feel helpless and alone, feeding the cycle. The abuse got worse and I hid it from everyone I knew, I was isolated and ate for comfort. I became overweight and this was another way he could humiliate me.

I left many times, only to return, and the cycle of abuse continued. I now lived in fear of someone I used to love.

Finally after five years of torture and abuse, I found the courage to leave. When I reached my lowest point,

I seemed to find my greatest strength. I knew when I ran out the door that day, after a traumatic beating, that I would never ever come back and it is a feeling I remember and cherish. I had finally found me again in all the pain, I knew I could make it back to my own life.

I have worked hard on respecting and loving me and it's a journey I continue today. I have experienced the trauma of abuse, the loneliness of isolation and the courage it takes to make it through.

And finally, when the time was right, I met Paul, the most wonderful man I have ever had the privilege to love. He was patient and he was kind and we were married in 2003. My hope in love continues.

THIS BODY IS MINE, NOT NERVOSA'S

AC, Dublin

When I was younger – maybe thirteen or fourteen – I had no idea how insidiously an eating disorder could creep into somebody's life, distorting their every thought and belief. I used to be scornful about the very notion of anorexia, thinking that it was surely a disease caused by stupidity. After all, how could people possibly think starving themselves was a good idea? There's no point in glossing over this – I was ignorant and harsh, and I'm very thankful that I'm not like that any more. Even so, I was happy enough with myself back then, albeit with as many insecurities and chinks in my armour as the next girl. I generally enjoyed my youth: I loved to draw, paint, act the eejit and bat my eyelashes at various unattainable boys in the hope of looking alluringly attractive.

At some stage – I cannot explain exactly how or why – a sense of shame and darkness came over me and I began to turn away from these positive and healthy aspects of my life. I have read and heard many accounts given by people whose eating disorders were prompted by horrific neglect and abuse, people whose childhoods were so much more painful than mine and rather than clarifying the cause of my own problem, these accounts almost made things more confusing for me. It seemed strange that I had never gone through any of these horrors, I had a happy childhood with a loving family...yet my eating disorder hit me just as suddenly and fiercely, reducing me to tears of despair every day. Maybe it was the isolation I frequently endured during my first two years of secondary school. Or maybe these things can't be explained in any logical or systematic way. Everybody reacts to events in different ways and what devastates one person might not be a big deal to another.

Even now, with the worst of my problems behind me and a brighter future stretching ahead, I find it hard to state aloud that cold scientific term 'anorexia/bulimia nervosa', as if there's still a part of me refusing to accept that either of those terms could possibly refer to me. I didn't want – and I never do want – to identify myself fully with the disease or believe it to be an unchangeable part of me. When I did finally accept the truth – that I had a serious problem with food – I simply began to think of my condition as 'it'. I later personified 'it' by imagining a demonic creature, 'Nervosa', warping my perception of myself, strangling my confidence and determined to silence the inner voice that told me that I was beautiful exactly as I was and worthy of love.

Nervosa first came to me when I was in fifth year, although of course I didn't realise who she was or what she intended to do to me. At first I began to experience vague thoughts about losing a bit of weight, then my thoughts turned into actions. It was unnoticeable at first – a skipped lunch here, an energetic long walk there – but before I knew it I became locked into a vicious cycle of deprivation, punishing exercise regimes, bingeing, purging, deprivation, exercise, bingeing…It went on and on for almost two years until I felt like a guinea pig running incessantly on its wheel, with no escape and no way of getting off. Whenever I think of the pain and worry my family and my friends endured as they watched me slowly self-destruct and the depth of their love for me even while this was going on, I know that I can never thank them enough. They stood by me time and time again and reminded me how beautiful I truly was and for ever will be, both inside and out.

The most important thing I learned while I was

teaching myself to eat properly again was to relax into the present moment, rather than torturing myself with unanswerable questions like: 'When did I become such an obsessive perfectionist?' or 'Why has my life ended up like this, with me sitting here trying to physically force myself not to run over to the dog and throw my perfectly healthy, nutritious dinner at his feet?' It took a lot of effort and, yes, more tears, before I was able to turn off those voices in my head and allow myself to take it one day, one minute, one second at a time.

Eventually I decided that Nervosa had run my life for long enough. For the first time in ages, I became more interested in considering the deeper questions of existence. I started to read books that dealt with spiritual and esoteric topics, books that made me question my own place in the world – and in doing so, I discovered another side to myself: a side that has never lost or gained as much as an ounce, never stressed itself out over what the future holds and always lives in the now. It is this presence that some people call God.

I use the word 'God' with some trepidation. For me, it still evokes a mental image of a judgemental old man who perches majestically on His throne of cloud, playing favourites with people's lives. Needless to say, I strongly doubt that this malevolent God exists. That kind of deity wouldn't deserve a scrap of anybody's respect, let alone their undying devotion and worship. But one thing I do believe – because I have experienced it to be true – is that we all have an unshakable core of beauty within us, a beauty so powerful and profound that we – that is to say, our egos, our shadow selves – are scared silly by it. We deny its existence, either consciously or unconsciously. We convince ourselves that we're worthless. We become disgusted by our emotions, our natural impulses and our own bodies. And when we stop caring for ourselves, we automatically become blind to the way our actions affect others. This was certainly what happened in my case. This is why I became obsessed with food, determined to deprive myself, punish myself, curse myself – even as my dismayed family and friends looked on, praying that I would one day regain my senses. I finally did so by recognising Nervosa as being nothing more than a liar.

Only when I stopped listening to Nervosa and started listening to my body did I begin to understand all that it could be. The human body can be fierce and aggressive, tender and gentle; strong but fragile; mesmerisingly complex but breathtaking in its simplicity. It is paradoxical. Mysterious. Miraculous.

But I, blinded by my fears and obsessions, wasn't grateful to have it. I deprived it of all the nutrients it desperately needed, I forced it to exercise for hours on end without a break and I was irritated by its cries for nourishment. I tried to convince myself that I didn't really have this desire for food. I was ashamed of it. I despised my body.

And still, despite the obstacles I constantly laid in its path, it valiantly continued to chug onwards, giving me the gift of life, hopeful that it would some day be treated with the love and care that it craved, that I would one day open my eyes and my heart to the joy and laughter to be found on the planet and that I would one day be profoundly grateful for my life and everyone in it. Until the end of my time on Earth, this amazing body of mine will be loyal, consistent, courageous. This construction of flesh and bone, blood and water is absolutely irrepressible!

I want to keep loving and understanding my body and I want to be in touch with my divine essence at every moment of every day. I want to be in touch with it as I eat my meals. I want to be in touch with it whenever I smile and listen to my siblings joke and squabble with one another. I want to be in touch with it each time a friend regales me with some hilarious anecdote and we both crease up, helpless with laughter. I deserve to live my life to the full. So does the Dalai Lama. So does Madonna. So does the drunkard whom everybody crosses the street to avoid. So does every single anorexic, bulimic, or compulsive eater who sees no way out of their tortured relationship with food.

To anyone who is suffering an eating disorder of any kind, I don't want to give the impression that I found recovery easy to achieve, because it certainly wasn't. It was the hardest thing I've ever done, without a doubt. I had to search deep inside myself and confront all the insecurities, guilt and pain I had accumulated throughout the years. And I do not now enjoy some kind of blissed-out, stress-free existence. Sometimes I'm more inclined to moan and sulk then to look for the inherent goodness in all sentient beings. Sometimes while I'm running late for some appointment or other, I don't keep an eye on the footpath and I end up falling flat on my face, the contents of my bag spilling out all over the street. Sometimes I put my foot in it and make some ill-advised remark, upsetting my nearest and dearest. Sometimes Nervosa sidles up to me and whispers that all this spiritual discovery lark is pointless – and by the way, I'm looking a bit chubby… So it's not as if all my troubles have disappeared in a puff of smoke. But

I know, without a shred of doubt, that I have enough strength to deal with whatever life throws at me. I tell Nervosa exactly where she can shove her nonsense. Whose body is it, anyway, Nervosa? Yours or mine? I get over my sulk and apologise to whoever I've offended. I pick myself up from the ground and dust myself off with as much dignity as I can muster.

If you are still grappling with Nervosa, still under her spell, then all I can say to you is: give up the fight. Really. When Nervosa starts up with one of her hysterical rants: 'You're useless, you look absolutely disgusting, you're a disgrace to everybody, a blot on the face of this Earth,' simply refuse to engage with her. Nervosa is a parasite. Without the vital attention and energy of her host – you – she cannot exist.

At some point, you will realise that the oppressive label of 'anorexic/bulimic/compulsive eater' that hangs around your neck does not define who you are, however much it may seem to. You are a loving, ineffably strong soul. And that soul has always been resting in the peaceful eye of your ego's self-constructed storm. Once you truly understand this, you will appreciate your body for all that it can do… and never again be vanquished by Nervosa.

These days I'm a college student with many obligations to fulfil, so I spend a great deal of my time rushing around like a headless chicken. But every night, before I go to sleep, I pray that everyone will open up to the love that has always dwelt in their hearts, waiting to be revealed.

JACK IRWIN

Jonathan Irwin, County Kildare

On 29 February 1996 my son Jack Irwin was born, a bonny bouncy baby.

Two days later Jack suffered a devastating trauma in the hospital's nursery and, although we'll never know for sure, it's probable that my little son died and was resuscitated.

What I do know for definite is that from that moment, my life changed for ever, just like Jack's and the rest of our family's. His brain was damaged, he could not swallow, he was blind and deaf and our dreams for him were shattered. From that day on, our duty as parents was to keep Jack warm, cosy and loved and we just had to get him home where he belonged.

The senior paediatrician was brutal and kind in his honesty. In the Ireland of 1996, there were no services for Jack beyond the hospital walls. Our only option, he said, was to pack Jack's little bag and abandon him in hospital; only then would the state step up and take care of him. We said, 'No,' to that option.

We brought Jack home, not knowing how or if we'd cope. We were in a real-life nightmare and still in shock.

Thankfully, the sun began to shine: a friend of a friend who was a nurse assembled a little team of friends and neighbours who became Jack's care team for his twenty-two months of life at home, a bitter-sweet mix of drugs, physio, cuddles and care. Jack just loved the bath. The water gave him comfort and a lift like nothing else. Once I heard him chuckle while the Grand National played out on TV. He couldn't see or hear but he sensed that big beautiful horse race somehow and he liked it. That chuckle is one I will cherish forever.

Jack's mum, Mary Ann, and I didn't want any other parents to walk this difficult path alone so we established the Jack and Jill Children's Foundation in Jack's name in 1997.

Today we support three hundred and twenty families all over the country with children like Jack. As one proud dad said to me recently, the poor doctors still try to measure their IQ and motor function and use harsh words like brain damage and developmental delay while trying to fit them into a box a long way from 'normal'. But where is the charisma measure for children like Jack and his son Alex? They can't look back and hold grudges and they don't worry about tomorrow; instead they live in the here and now, crying when they are in pain and smiling when they're cosy again. These children, he said, are the closest thing we'll ever see to the face of God.

I agree with that proud dad. Our Jack and Jill babies, who live in every community in Ireland, may not kick a ball or do a crossword but they touch a part of your heart that nobody else can ever reach.

Jack was the turning point in my life. His legacy lives on through Jack and Jill. My wise little boy shows me the way and marches me back up that hill again.

A Second Chance at Life

Michael (Finny) Collum, County Mayo

I was extremely fit. I used to train three nights a week
– football and running – and I cycled everywhere.
Then all of a sudden I started to get tired when I was
cycling around town. It felt strange. I was also losing
weight. So I went to the doctor and told him I was
having some problems. I was working as a labourer in
Sligo Corporation at the time. The doctor referred me
to the local hospital and I was diagnosed with asthma.
This was in December 1987.

I went back to work in January of 1988 and on
my first day back, I wasn't able to do a job I would
normally have done. I got weak. I went back to the
doctor and he referred me to Dublin, so by mid-
January I was in St James's having tests and more
tests. The head doctor was called in to have a look
at the tests. I remember two women sitting out in
A&E saying, 'It's great when you have money; you get
the top guys.' They thought I was a private patient –

everybody was so interested in the results of my tests.

They said I would have to have more tests and asked if I had ever worked in a mine. No, but I had been a plumber for seven years. My lungs were black when they should have been soft and pink. I had smoked but had given them up a year previously. I was twenty-six years old.

I was sent to Peamount Hospital, which worked to my advantage. I credit Dr Paul Kelly with saving me. For the next year I was in and out of Peamount and Sligo hospitals. My ability to breath was rapidly declining. A biopsy was done on my lungs and I was told I had emphysema. The doctors were telling me to live with it but Dr Paul Kelly said, 'No way, there has to be something else.'

I went to Newcastle Hospital in England in March 1989 to undergo tests for a lung transplant. For the next eleven months I was very close to death. I couldn't walk ten yards without getting breathless, I weighed six stone and a breeze could knock me over. The final diagnosis was bronchiolitis obliterans. This is apparently the end result of a lot of lung diseases.

In February 1990 I had a heart and lung transplant in Newcastle Hospital. Six similar operations had been done at about the same time. Four of these patients had died and the fifth was sick in hospital. There was

50

er the truth but I was prepared to take

peration was a success. The minute I woke up had no problem breathing and within three days of the operation I was on the exercise bike. I left hospital on 9 April. Coming back home on the plane I got frightened because I felt I was so far away if I needed help. I convinced myself that I was not going to need it, that I would be fine.

I couldn't go back to my job in Sligo Corporation. What else could I work at? I had left school at thirteen. I didn't know how I was going to earn a living. I went back to education. I went on a VTOS course and did my Leaving Certificate Applied. I went on to Sligo Regional College where over two years I did a Certificate in Social Studies and received the North Western Health Board Medal for highest overall grade average in class that year. Then I achieved my National Diploma in Social Studies. Then job-hunting. My first job was as information officer with the Markievicz Unemployment Centre. Today I am a social care leader in a group home.

After seven years I rejected the transplant. It was touch and go on many occasions for me. There was new medication just on the market. The irony was that the medication was not available in Ireland, although it was manufactured in Kerry!

I got a second chance at life, I changed careers and I remarried in 2004. I still attend the Mater Hospital. I keep relatively fit with walking and gardening. Most days I don't think that twenty years ago I had a heart and lung transplant. I notice that some people are afraid after this operation, afraid that something will happen. They won't go into crowds or pubs. I just live my life to the full. I will be thankful for the rest of my life to the families who donate organs – who have such great generosity and empathy when they are suffering the worst nightmare of their lives.

Fours Walls and Four Children

Agnes Johnson, Dublin

When I look back on it now, I was only six weeks married when my father was killed off his bike. Three years later my mother died. My husband did shift work and the babies came along. I had three girls and one boy. After the birth of my youngest, I was coming back from the school one day and something came over me. I became very frightened.

I then started to became fearful of going out. If I walked down to the garden gate the perspiration would pour off me. I used to think I was having a brain haemorrhage. A good friend of mine started to do all my shopping for me. The kids would laugh at me as I was saying things backwards because I was so uptight. I could go out in the car with my husband because there was safety in the car and I could come back home if I got really bad. I explained to the priest why I had to stay at the back of the church during Mass and his response was, 'There's thousands like you.' Before all this happened, my husband and children and I used to go on camping holidays in Eastern Europe – in 1985 we even camped in Russia. Eventually my life became 'four walls and four children'.

The doctor told me I was having panic attacks and that I could go on tablets. Once I knew what was happening, I think I got some power over it. I didn't want to take tablets. I noticed I could work myself up to it and began to teach myself to take deep breaths. Counselling was not as available then as it is now but I was beginning to learn that it was mind over matter. For the children's sake, I pushed myself when I was asked to help out with some fundraising with our local scouts. I stayed with the scouts and in time became a Beaver leader.

One day I went to the Mansion House to an alternative medicine exhibition and it changed my life. I got talking to the girl on the Red Cross Stand and she said they were looking for volunteers for their therapeutic hand-care programme. After I did the course I started to work in Donnycarney and Beaumont social centre as a Red Cross therapeutic hand-care volunteer. Time passed and I become an instructor with the Red Cross. At a recent Reynaud's Awareness Day in St Vincent's Hospital, there were many very specialised people and I was there amongst them. When I was about to get up and talk in front of all these knowledgeable people I started to shake. I had to have a good talk with myself. I said to myself, 'I don't know their subject and they don't know mine.'

The Red Cross also trains people in camouflage make-up. This service was developed in England during the Falklands War. Trained volunteers show sufferers what make-up to use and the best way to apply it in order to camouflage raspberry stains, burns and skin discolouration. The make-up lasts for sixteen hours and is waterproof.

Today I am Director for Community Activities for the Irish Red Cross in the Dublin area.

I'm glad now I listened to my friend when she said, 'You'd want to get up, you're like Cinderella there, and one day your kids will be gone.'

SOMETHING AMAZING
IS HAPPENING TO ME

Maeve Witherow, County Tipperary

My name is Maeve and I am forty years old and have spina bifida. I want to tell you about something amazing that happened to me.

In April 1970, my parents were delighted with their new arrival, their first girl. But their joy and excitement were dimmed when they were told that their little girl had spina bifida. Shock, hurt and, of course, feelings of, 'Why us?' floated around their heads. Both my parents are very positive and even during this awful time they supported each other, gathered their inner strength and decided they would deal with it as best they could.

And so they have. Our mother said that if their daughter lived until she was ten, twenty or even older, they would make sure that I grew up independently and help me to live as normal a life as possible. So from those positive thoughts my life's journey began.

Growing up with spina bifida was not easy. I've

had four major operations and countless visits to different hospitals, visits that became a way of life for me. Poor feeling in my legs has always been a problem. A simple knock or bump can give rise to cuts or sores and the simple feeling of being cold all the time causes its own problems. I can remember sitting on a radiator and because I couldn't feel the heat, I got serious burns without feeling any sense of pain. My legs, although functional, have always been on the wobbly side. Standing still has never been easy.

School. What can I say about it? I managed to get through despite being absent a lot and I succeeded in getting my Leaving Certificate. Not being able to join my siblings and classmates in physical activities was difficult and when I tried to join, I invariably fell over and became the object of name-calling and ridicule by some. I know I am one of the lucky ones with spina bifida. I am able to walk, I have a job and I lead a fairly normal life. I succeeded in passing my driving test the first time and I drive to work most days.

Anthony and I have been married for thirteen years but not being able to have a baby has upset me greatly. After I had been feeling sorry for myself for a few months, a friend suggested that I should try complementary medicine, so after a bit of research I began to do so.

After a year or so of going to Mella Ryan Ring at An Dúiche Holistic Health Centre in Tipperary for different treatments ranging from reflexology to reiki and massage, I did not get pregnant but something strange happened to me. A sense of feeling started to come into my legs. It was a very strange feeling and in some ways a scary one. Over the next few months I noticed that I could stand up straight without wobbling. The circulation in my legs had also improved.

For the first time in my life I started to feel confident and good about myself. Maybe the best part is that I no longer need a caliper. I was being fitted for one in Cashel and on the fourth fitting the man seemed exasperated and said to me, 'Maeve, I've been making these for years and there is something very wrong here.' He threw the caliper aside and said to me, 'You don't need one.'

That has given me the ability to face the future with a sense of excitement. One thing that my treatments have taught me is the I need to keep positive. I know I don't walk straight but I have started to improve.

Who knows? Only God knows what will happen next!

The One-Flipper Print

Pauline Beades, Irish Seal Sanctuary

The silver sheen on the coat of the grey seal pup belied the suffering and injuries underneath. She had been hauled up on Garretstown beach, County Cork, a weaned but very young pup, emaciated and holding a hugely swollen front flipper away from her body, trying desperately to relieve the throbbing pain. She was spotted by some beach walkers who rang the Irish Seal Sanctuary for advice and we made the decision that she needed to be brought to the sanctuary for care.

Catching a wild animal can be a challenge at the best of time but an animal in such pain is an added challenge. The volunteers tried their best not to make contact with the obviously painful flipper but avoiding the dangers of her jaws while avoiding inflicting further pain was not an easy balance to reach. Finally the little fighter was contained. A tube was fed down into her stomach and warm, comforting rehydration fluids were poured into her to help her deal with the stress of capture and transport, not to mention to replace the fluids she would have lost as a result of starvation and pain.

The seal, whom we named Pat, was given antibiotics for the flipper infection but it was apparent that this was no normal infection and she was brought to the veterinary hospital in UCD. The results were not good. The infection had spread into the bone and would, if not stopped, move up into the skeleton and eventually kill her. There was a very stark choice: either Pat had to be euthanised or her front flipper had to be amputated.

The removal of a front flipper was not known to have been done before; it was a ground-breaking operation with no guarantee of Pat's being able to return to the wild afterwards.

The decision was agonising. The Irish Seal Sanctuary does not keep captive animals and putting a wild grey seal that could not survive back in the wild was unthinkable but Pat was in every other way a strong healthy animal with a great zest for life.

It was decided that if anyone could beat this, Pat could. She came through the anaesthetic well and the rehabilitation process began in earnest. She rewarded our confidence in her by eating a healthy meal a few hours after the surgery! She was a very strong animal and tending the wound was challenging, to say the least, but finally the point was reached where she could be put into a pool with other seals to begin to develop the competitive instinct she needed to survive in the wild.

Initially, if anyone strange arrived, Pat played dead, obviously nervous about her abilities to get away.

Soon she began to gain confidence and swim strongly, matching her pool mates. As she would have needed two flippers to change direction, she simply spun over on her back, using the remaining flipper to control her direction. We finally saw the day approach when she could be returned to the wild. However we wanted to be sure she would be able to hunt, so we put her into a lake with wild trout. Whoosh, she took off and hunted like a professional. She caught herself a trout, proving that her rehabilitation was complete.

Pat was released into Dublin Bay at Bull Island. She is hunting and hanging out with the grey seal colony in that area. We know this because her one-flipper print is often spotted on the beach there by wildlife wardens.

SEVEN YEARS CLEAN

Anonymous

I was the second youngest of seven children. My father was a heavy drinker. My mother was ill quite a lot. There wasn't much guidance or direction and there was always friction in the home, which would have impacted on my schooling. This is how it was throughout my childhood and teenage years.

I had a problem with learning that was un-recognised. I acted out a lot as a child, especially in school. My mind would always be elsewhere – distracted – and I'd feel inadequate because I had difficulty learning. I was often in trouble and would be put at the back of the class or sent out of the classroom. Sometimes, I'd be sent to pick up the papers in the yard and I would wish that I was back in the class and feel even worse about myself. This is where I learned to escape from my thoughts and feelings, through humour and fantasy.

I left school at fifteen. The culture of the time

where I lived on the northside of Dublin was to hang out with the lads in the summer-time. The first experience of getting out of my mind was sniffing petrol and cannisters of gas. Anything for a laugh or a buzz. The first time I took alcohol I was about seven or eight. My father would give me Guinness and he'd make a laugh about me drinking Guinness. It felt good to have this interaction with my father as there wasn't much of it while I was growing up.

The first time I got drunk was at the age of fourteen or fifteen when a friend took a bottle of Cognac from his house. I drank more than everyone else. I was the one who got sick or arrested. I always seemed to take things to the limit. We hung around with older lads in the area who were more advanced in their drinking and robbing and we looked up to them. We'd hang around the local shops during the day and scheme and scam for money for that night. We drank cider in the summer and wine in the winter to keep us warm.

I was getting into more and more trouble. The highlight of the night was to get chased by the Gardaí. This was fun at the start but it became more of a burden as we got older. We used to get bits of work on the milk and bread vans but we'd lose the jobs when we didn't turn up because of our drinking and drugging. We'd do a bit of robbing in the local shops, the local factories. We progressed to smoking hash and before we knew it we were selling and dealing it between ourselves. When we were eighteen we thought we were great, we were able to get the dole.

As I look back on it now I think it was very sad.

I was always dreaming, in a fantasy world. I had a radio I got as a present and I would listen to music on it. I dreamt about the future – how rich and powerful I was going to be – and that my mother and father were happier. I used to see pictures of Ethiopia and the Third World and I would feel for these people and always said I would love to do something for them some day. My next-door neighbour looked out for me and gave me some direction. She would steer me in the direction of a bit of work and she had great heart for the community. But I drank and smoked hash most nights.

My drinking and drugging progressed until, at about the age of twenty-three, I was introduced to DF118s, as the drinking wasn't working any more. It didn't take away how I used to think about myself and my life. Even though I was a quiet and loving guy it was coming out of me in other ways. I'd get nasty at times and did things I shouldn't do. When I'd wake up I couldn't wait till night-time. When I started taking these I fell in love with them. There was a doctor in

Dublin who would give scripts for them in return for cash.

Then I remember the fella who introduced me to MSTs (NAPS is the street name). I saw him injecting the tablets and I asked him to do it for me. I injected my first drug in 1993-4. I alternated between NAPS and heroin. At the time heroin was £40 a bag and this stuff was £25. My dad had cancer around the same time I started to dabble and I used to rob his tablets. Before I knew it I was strung out. That's when I started to get heavily addicted. I was sticking needles in myself every day. My family found out and I went in to Beaumont Hospital to detox. After six weeks there I got clean. I was asked to go to follow-on treatment but I wouldn't go. Thought I'd be OK. Going back to the same situation with no supports my chances of staying clean were not good.

I hated life and how I felt about myself. Here I was in my mid-twenties with no purpose in life, no goals and no future. I got back into the cycle of addiction. I burnt all my bridges with family and neighbours. I hadn't it in me to rob at this stage because I had had a taste of prison and I didn't like it. It broke my mother's heart seeing me like this and she and would often say, 'He's going to be found dead.' I was using addiction as a way of coping but it was causing me more pain.

I used to go to Merchant's Quay needle exchange and they asked me if I would like to do their residential programme, which I did. It was great just to get eight hours sleep, wash and eat properly and to be happy, joyous and free After finishing this programme, once again I thought I could do it myself and didn't avail of aftercare. I didn't want to accept I was an addict. Before long I was at it again. My family was baffled and confused: why would I do this to them and to myself?

I went on methadone in 2000 and I thought this would fix me. In that culture I was introduced to different drugs and I spiralled downhill and as a result got hepatitis-C. My health deteriorated rapidly. I weighed five stone and I was walking around on a crutch. My body was full of abscesses from needles. I developed a cocaine habit at this stage. To get that drug I did things I would never have dreamed of doing. I did things against all my morals and values. Eventually, I was admitted to a psychiatric unit and while I was there I reflected and remembered what it was like to be free from drugs. In bed that night I prayed to God to help me. I didn't want to be like this.

During this time I was in and out of my mother's home and more or less homeless. A counsellor I was seeing got me into transitional housing in Focus

Ireland. I was still going around on my crutch and was very thin. But things started to improve. Something inside me told me things were going to work out. I now had my own place. I attended a day programme, it was something to do and you got your dinner every day. They saw something in me that I couldn't see in myself. My desire to get clean got stronger. I stopped taking street drugs. My methadone come down and the anti-depressants and Valium as well. I reduced to 40 mls of methadone, the requirement for a residential detox, and I went to Cuan Dara in Cherry Orchard Hospital. When I was there members of Narcotics Anonymous came up and shared their experiences of strength and hope. I knew some of them from a few years earlier and it gave me great hope. I hoped I could do what they were doing. It inspired me to keep going. Because of the way I grew up I had no hope or confidence but I found it in myself and others. I felt God worked through them.

My obsession with using lifted, yet I was fearful of it. I went straight back to the day programme after treatment and they were very helpful and supportive. I started to grow and develop as a person. I found my voice and my confidence and self-esteem grew. I started to accept who I was and know my strengths. I started to see things clearly and to grow spiritually. I joined NA and after thirty days clean I got a badge. I felt brilliant. It was my first real achievement.

After attending two day-programmes I needed to learn how to live in the real world and be responsible. All my life I had escaped as a class clown, by listening to the radio and by using drink and drugs but today I am learning to live in reality. I did FETAC courses and became a volunteer in the addiction services. I went on to college and have just graduated with my diploma in addiction studies.

I have a great desire to help other people with addictions and people in general. My dream of helping those in the Third World has been realised because for the last three years I have gone on mission trips. During my recovery I became very drawn to study Christianity. My perception of Christianity has changed: I learned that Jesus was a great leader and a servant.

I achieved many things over the past seven years: my life has changed and I have changed amazingly. As a result of my studies, life started to pick up and now I have my own apartment and a nice car. I work in a recovery centre and I am a board member of an addiction service. It's not too long since I was isolated in my addiction, in darkness, in despair, at death's door with no hope, no future, no life. Today I am seven years clean and free from active addiction, with a purpose and a future. God's love worked through people to get me to this place.

'The Journey'

Mary Hunt, County Roscommon

A friend once gave me a poem called 'Wild Geese' by the American poet, Mary Oliver. The point my friend was making was that all you need to do in life is be yourself. Good advice indeed. It was not that particular poem that came to mean so much to me but another poem by Mary Oliver called 'The Journey', that I discovered during a time of growth in my life. It was also a hard time but that is neither here nor there. 'The Journey' helped me to believe more in myself, in my own judgment and choices. This is the story of my own personal journey.

I had my first breakdown at the age of twenty-six and afterwards the psychiatric services put me in touch with some courses. I took the only art-related one then available, a course in graphic design. It was funded for five years and I thought that for that period I would be safe.

At the end of the five years I appeared to be doing

well and when a job came up in the organisation where I had been training I took it. But I immediately began to become unwell. This was compounded by the fact that we had some training days on mental health during which I heard things that made me afraid to take my medication. I attended a second information day. Some of the things said struck home because they were descriptions, word for word, of my own personal experience. The phrase that tugged at something inside me and made my cry was, '…people who don't have, and might never have had, a sense of themselves.' This was the very thing I didn't have. I would say I'm a sensitive and shy person. I can be very hard on myself but there is much about me that is good. My problem is that I have always had and still have trouble believing it.

It was during this time that I looked up the web on Mary Oliver and discovered the poem called 'The Journey', which is about relying on and trusting oneself. The line that struck a chord with me was, 'There was a new voice//which you slowly// recognized as your own'. I suppose I was developing a genuine sense of self.

After that I became very unwell, I had my second breakdown and was diagnosed with schizophrenia. I was hospitalised and treated.

During my time in recovery, I built on this new sense of self. With a little more confidence I have been able to hold down a part-time job and develop my hobbies and interests. I have been stable now for seven years. I will never come off medication again, as I have come to terms with needing it, but I have learned to avoid what stresses me and concentrate on what I am able to do and what I have. I have a loving family, a supportive partner and a very good life. You can imagine my joy the day the consultant told me that I was to be discharged from the psychiatric services into the care of my GP as I had been well for so long.

When I was given the poem I wrote to Mary Oliver, asking for a copy of her book for my friend. Recently I wrote to her asking for a copy for a lovely person I have only recently come to appreciate. Myself!

I'm My Own Boss Now

Corina Martinez, Sasama, El Viejo, Nicaragua

I used to live in fear of my partner, who beat me whenever he wanted and with whatever was at hand and also abused me sexually. He beat my children, four of whom were not his, and when I intervened to stop him he would go for me too. I had to ask permission to leave the house. I didn't know how to read and write and thought there was nothing I could do to change my life.

Then APADEIM (Association for the Holistic Development of Women) offered the women in my community literacy classes and I started going, bringing my baby girl along. He used to beat me for leaving the house but I kept on going and now I can read and write.

APADEIM gave us training in gender and gender-based violence and they also distributed leaflets on women's rights. I realised that I had rights and needed to value myself and not take my cue from him when he said I was worthless. When I went to the training sessions and he wanted to stop me I would say to him, 'You can't tell me what to do,' and little by little he stopped beating me for it. I also prevented him from hitting the children I have by other fathers. Now I deal with them myself. And in this I have also changed. I never used to hit them but I didn't treat them well and was always on top of them just because they were kids. Now I realise this is wrong and I speak to them with affection. My daughters are big now and I don't want them to go through what I suffered.

APADEIM also gave me a donation of corrugated iron. This allowed me to make a roof for a house, so I moved out of my partner's house. Now I live under my own roof and I'm my own boss.

At the end of the training sessions on gender-based violence I received a police certificate accrediting me as a legal facilitator for women who have experienced violence. When a woman wants to report violence she comes to me and I go to the police and the social services and make the report on behalf of the woman. Because I have a certificate I am accepted by the police and the social workers and they always treat me with respect, take my reports seriously and act on them. This gives me more confidence and also means that in the community I am considered a force to be reckoned with and nobody demeans me any more. I am a completely different person because of the training I received from APADEIM and I thank God that they came to work in my community.

APADEIM implements a gender-based violence programme in El Viejo, Nicaragua, funded by Trócaire.

What I Was So Fearful Of Now Brings Me the Most Joy

James, Dublin

My earliest memory is of no connection. My dad was distant and my mother used to put me in the spotlight. I were always wrong and there was always a comment. My father was an alcoholic and he was more violent when he was sober. I would be in bed and the violence would start. I was aware that things were not comfortable at home and I stayed out of the house a lot. At ten I witnessed my father trying to rape and kill my mother.

I was never comfortable around people. I wasn't able to be in people's company even if I knew them for years. I would scan people's faces, always alert to see if their expression was changing. I started drinking at sixteen and taking recreational drugs: LSD, cannabis and speed. The older brothers of some of my friends were harder into the drink and we started to associate with them.

One day I thought I was having a bad LSD trip.

I felt pure fear. I went into the bathroom and threw water on myself. I looked in the mirror and my pupils were so dilated that there was no colour in my eyes. I was having a panic attack. I went to the hospital and they gave me tranquillisers.

I did my Leaving Certificate and a Post-Leaving Certificate course. I had no relationship with my parents or siblings so I went to live with an aunt and broke down and didn't go outside her door for six months. I was paranoid and isolated between my two ears. I was terrified to go to the GP, I thought I would be sectioned and that he would put me in St Brendan's. I couldn't even go to bed from fear and stayed in the sitting-room with the TV on. When I calmed down I went to the GP. I didn't want to go on medication so I was referred to a counsellor. I was full of self-doubt. I didn't just drink to take the edge off things, I drank not to feel, until I had blackouts. I couldn't work 9-5 because I couldn't relate to people in an office. For twelve years I worked on-site in a job where I went around to various companies.

The drinking and the panic attacks were getting worse. I would be drenched in sweat going to the car. My self-esteem got lower and lower. I was becoming more isolated and the desperation was getting worse. I never developed relationships with women and the on-site work was getting harder. I began to take cocaine. I couldn't talk to people or form relationships. I couldn't accept where I came from, how I looked and that I couldn't relate to people.

I went to a party at the house of my closest friend in the country. The party went on for five days. While he was in bed I got a shotgun in the house and went into the woods and put the barrel in my mouth but I hadn't the strength to pull the trigger. I never took cocaine again after that.

My job got harder and I couldn't go to meetings or the Christmas party or any social events. I didn't like going into big offices with thirty or forty people. I thought people were looking at me 24/7. I couldn't go into coffee shops or meet people for lunch. If someone looked at me I would sweat as if I'd run a marathon. I used to wear two to three T-shirts to try and disguise it. I thought everyone could see my anxiety. Friends fell away. I tried to get my own place a few times but I would end up back home, back to the tensions between me and my dad.

A friend was getting married and he invited me to the wedding. I'd get the odd phone call and as the wedding was getting nearer the calls would come more frequently. Other friends were calling me too. I wouldn't answer the phone calls or the texts. I couldn't listen to them asking me why I wasn't coming.

Then I went to New York with a drinking buddy. I have never been in a city with so many people and felt so alone and disconnected. We were drinking in shitholes. The scale of life there – the tourists in Times Square. I could see I was so removed. All I wanted to do was throw myself in front of a subway train but I thought of the consequences for my friend.

It began to dawn on me that the pain of getting better and that facing things couldn't be as bad as this.

I found out about the Social Anxiety Clinic in the Mater Hospital and put my name down for the course there. I waited one and half years for a place. I started to see counsellors about the age of twenty-three and I cried for years. I still see a counsellor on a weekly basis. I was in a vicious cycle for years because I could not accept my childhood. I could not accept that I feel shy. I never wanted to feel that way. I found myself enrolling on a course in Chrysalis in Wicklow called 'Breakthrough: Transforming Codependency'. The facilitator on this course told me the way things were. If I continued to live the life I was living I would probably commit suicide in two years or end up in a psychiatric hospital. It was one or the other. Nobody was ever as direct as this with me before. The course was the scariest thing I ever did but it was beautiful.

Last year I started a course in the Mater Hospital which was run by the senior psychologist, Odhran McCarthy. When I walked into the room and looked at the other people there, they all seemed so normal. It is a cognitive behaviour course and it is not about looking into your past. I talked about my dad for years in counselling.

It is a three-month course that you attend on a weekly basis and there are ten people in the group. It is very structured. Acceptance is the key. I learnt that I can be nervous and that it will pass. You let a feeling ride itself out. It's like a surf wave: it comes and goes and you will go from a high anxiety to a more relaxed state.

I learned that I am not the centre of attention. I learnt that I never wanted to feel anxious or scared. I was self-centred in a self-destructive way. To others this can appear to be aloof. We did a role-play of a high-anxiety situation and it was videoed. When you saw the video you talked about how you thought you did and the group looked at how you did. Every one of us who did the video was very critical of ourselves – the self-critic was very strong. Even stunning-looking women could not see that they were attractive.

Last year I took my last drink. I knew I couldn't drink safely any more. My tolerance was gone and it took very little for me to black-out. I rang a friend I knew who had stopped drinking and went along to AA. I felt at home in AA. A lot of people there suffer from restlessness and unease. AA is the best therapy but I wouldn't recommend the path I took to get there. I act as secretary at meetings. Before I would have rather taken a bullet or jumped out the window.

I have found living with social anxiety is about having a tool kit. I'm so glad now that I didn't take medication and that I will not be on antidepressants for the rest of my life. I still have in-between days. Things do change. Things do pass. I do a form of meditation called mindfulness. I meditate and sit with my feelings. I am thankful to be here. It is great to be able to say, 'I'm not perfect, I'm OK as I am.' And mean it. I'm not so preoccupied with myself.

One of my biggest regrets is that when I was thirty-four my brother asked me to be his best man but I turned him down point blank. I never gave him a reason or excuse, just the word, 'No.' I wouldn't be able to face standing up in front of people and being in the spotlight for the day. This just proves how much people with social anxiety are preoccupied with what they believe people think about them.

The Sanctuary, which was founded by Sister Stanislaus, organises a volunteering services whereby you visit patients in St Brendan's. I'm not doing it for my social anxiety, I'm doing it because when I reach out I get so much back. What I was so fearful of in life – people – is now what brings me the most joy. I go in there and they know me by name and I get a great sense of connection from that. The less I think about me the happier I am. If I wait to be more comfortable going out, it will never happen.

When the course in the Mater was finished I decided to do the follow-up group and a number of my buddies on the course said they would too. But all my buddies didn't come. Do I go or do I run? I went in and I was asked to go and talk to people about being in the follow-up group. My normal reaction would have been to say, 'No.' But I did it. I told them that they wouldn't be fixed in three months, whatever the anxiety was, but that they would enjoy a non-judgemental atmosphere in the follow-up group. I am still in that group today.

And I have just been accepted into Dublin City University to do a degree course in psychology.

I Don't Do Floors

Valerie Bowe, Waterford

My mother gave birth to nine children, two of whom died in infancy. She was a marvellous woman and a great businesswoman. She had her own shop until her fifth child was born and she was great in the kitchen too: she was a super cook; made her own jams; pickled onions and crab-apple jelly. She preserved eggs in a big saucepan under the sink, in some solution called 'water glass'. At that time eggs were very expensive and scarce in winter and she preserved them for the Christmas cakes and puddings. She could turn her hand to sewing as well and did smocking on dresses. But one thing she did not do – she didn't do floors.

My auntie Bridie always told this story about my mother. She knew the time my father was coming home and the exact moment he would put the key in the door. So she got a great big bar of Sunlight soap, a scrubbing brush, a bucket and newspapers to kneel on. The scene was set. Our house was unusual in that you had to pass through one room to get to the other: you walked through the hall, then through the dining room to get to the kitchen at the back of the house. If all the doors were left open you could see straight into the kitchen from the hall door.

My mother left all the doors open, knelt down on the newspaper beside the bucket, soap and scrubbing brush and waited for my father to turn the key in the front door. When he did, all he saw was his wife in the kitchen, bent over a bucket, scrubbing vigorously.

He was taken aback. 'Jesus, Kitty,' he exclaimed, 'I never want to see you on your hands and knees like that. That's terrible.'

'Well, Danny,' my mother said, getting up off her knees, 'I could do with someone to clean the floors.'

For years, Kathleen Dunne cleaned our floors, beautifully.

21 JULY 2003

Anonymous

In the end, I would have licked it off the floor. Drink. This substance that I had always loathed and feared now held me in its vice-like grip.

My active alcoholism was a short-lived but savage period of my life. It turned me into a horrendously unstable, emotionally vulnerable, frightened, worried and totally irrational child-woman. For a period spanning three years, in my mid-thirties, I had virtually no control over my drinking. Prior to that I could be classified as a social drinker with a very healthy respect for alcohol. I was always mindful of what drink can do to people and was determined that I would be in control of it and not the other way around.

Now, looking back, I believe that drink was just a symptom of a deeper malaise. In its true meaning 'alcoholism' equals 'alcohol' and 'ism' and I had all the isms! Fear and worry are two of the biggest enemies of the soul and most alcoholics suffer terribly from these twin evils. Now I think that, for me, it was always going to end in tears, oceans of tears.

Once the real spark of my inherent alcoholism was ignited, it spiralled in a rapid and frightening manner. I escaped into a bottle. I drank, mostly alone: in my bedroom, in my car, in my office, in hotel rooms, solitary and hellish. I drank in the mornings, in the afternoon, in the evening, in the night and all through the night. That I had a thriving career, wonderful friends, a great background, education, looks and talents was utterly meaningless to me as I sank deeper and deeper into a liquid pool that was slowly drowning me.

The things that I swore would never happen to me, happened. I was arrested twice for drunk-driving. I was seen publicly drunk and disoriented. I collapsed in public. I missed work and totally ignored my commitments. It is nearly impossible to convey the abject terror and darkness that surrounded me.

The summer of 2003 is one that I will never ever forget and always want to remember. It was a beautiful summer, wonderfully warm and balmy, and the last one I spent in a drunken stupor. The sound of children laughing, people mowing their lawns, getting on with life – all was lost to me as I was lost.

My life was in flames and nothing could dampen that inferno.

My rock-bottom came one morning as I came to on my bedroom floor and raised an empty bottle to my lips. There was nothing left. I begged God for help. Thankfully, I always have had wonderful faith and strangely, despite all, this never deserted me.

That evening I ran to my first AA meeting. The people I met were warm and welcoming and their stories were familiar.

The first few months of sobriety were painful and hard reality. Life can be tough and stopping drinking is not a panacea. I still have days when things are difficult, stressful and chaotic. That's life. We all have days like that. The difference is that I am handling them without jumping into a bottle. I love my life now. Little did I know when I stumbled into my first AA meeting that in time I would get my peace of mind back, my career back on track, my driving licence back and, most important of all, meet the love of my life there. It truly is a wonderful life.

ADDICTED TO ADDICTS

Vera, Dublin

A woman's story of a husband's drinking and a daughter's heroin addiction.

At the age of sixteen I met Tom and fell in love. We did the usual things and went out but it was always to the pub. I did not think too much about this at the time as all my friends were doing the same. By the age of twenty-one we were married. We didn't make any real plans: we just went with the flow. We did not have much money but there was always money for drink.

I was unaware that there was a problem; I thought my life was normal. There were a lot of rows, especially when Tom was drunk, physical and, worst of all, verbal abuse. I had low self-esteem.

Four years later we had our first child, Sam. I hoped that life would be different and promises were made but never lasted long. I was sad and lonely and on my own a lot. Tom always came home with drink on him. If I said anything the verbal abuse would start. I learned to keep my mouth shut. There were years of abuse, hurt, fear and frustration.

Then our second child Ann was born. I hoped again that this child would change things but the quiet times did not last long. Tom was also suicidal. He always seemed to have a hold on me: the verbal abuse, the lies, the suicide attempts and his controlling behaviour. I had no life and I did not know who I was.

When I confronted my husband about his drinking and suggested that he might have a problem, he denied it. Shortly after this he overdosed on sleeping pills. I lived in fear; if I tried to change anything, the threat of suicide was always there. One night I rang AA and cried down the phone. They asked me to go to the Hanley Centre in Dún Laoghaire. A week later I went and it was a start. When I told my husband that I was going to AA he said, 'I'm glad that you're doing this for me.'

Over the years different things happened. My eldest daughter, Sam, found her father in the garage with the hose over the exhaust pipe. She was fourteen. Tom ended up in St John of God's for a few weeks. Even then I felt guilty; I felt that everything was my fault. It did not take long for Tom to get back to his old ways. I never felt that the children, our home or I were important enough to Tom for him to change.

It took twenty-three years of verbal abuse, lies, frustration, anger, fear, denial, pain, hurt, low self-esteem and walking on eggshells to get this man out of the family home. This would be the start of a new life. No more walking on eggshells. Life was good – or so I thought.

My youngest daughter Ann was having problems in school. She was fifteen when her father left so I felt guilty about that too, that it was my fault my daughter was having problems. I thought maybe I should take my husband back to make Ann happy. I thought maybe Ann suffered from depression.

Now that I did not have the alcoholic to focus on I focused on my daughter, trying to make things right for her. I was unaware what the problem was. It was five years later that I found out that Ann was a heroin user. I knew that Ann smoked dope but to find out that she was using heroin was unbelievable. The lies and stories, the familiar feelings: it all came back. The way I found out about my daughter was that she took an overdose of pills and ended up in hospital, and I took on the role of carer, enabler, of fear and guilt, of walking on egg shells. I was beginning to wonder who the addict was, if I was addicted to addicts and why this was happening to me.

Ann went on a methadone programme with the

help of our family doctor. I felt my daughter not only was on methadone but might have been using. One day Ann said, 'I'm sick of this; I don't want to be like this.' The next day I got the phone book out and rang drug information in Pearse Street. The lady said there should be a centre near to where we lived but I didn't want my daughter going somewhere close to home. There is a lot of shame and disappointment when you have a user of drugs in your home.

I rang Haniel in Sandyford, now know as Dún Laoghaire Rathdown Community Addiction Team and made an appointment to go up to see them two days later. I called them my angels. It was the first time I got real help and I let them help. In two weeks they got Ann into the Lantern for a six-weeks detox. It was great for me not to have to worry about my daughter. I also started going to counselling for myself and to the family support group once a week. I was starting to become more aware and was getting the support I had needed for so long. I was learning more about addiction and how it affects other members of the family. I learned not to walk in my daughter's shoes.

Ann came home after doing only a week in detox and used again. A few months later she went back to the Lantern and did the full six weeks but came out and used again. Months later she did six weeks in Cuan Dara and used again when she came home. Ann ended up back in contemplation on the wheel of change and in my own way so did I. I realised that I had been living with addiction all my adult life.

I have come a long way on my journey. Thanks to the help I got from the family support group my life has change a great deal. I helped the group to make a quilt and they decided to make it more positive than negative because there is always hope. I put symbols on the quilt to represent the males and females who have passed away through drug abuse, hoping I would never have to put a symbol of my own daughter on the quilt.

To educate myself I did a course on addiction studies in ARC (Addiction Response, Crumlin), to gain more knowledge and understanding and to find out more about different drugs and their effects on the individual. I learned about how I enabled my husband and my daughter in their addictions and about family crisis. New doors opened up for me. I became aware of how alcohol and drugs affect the family and the user. The patterns and the behaviours are similar. It's never too late to change and live in a happy and safe environment.

Sam has never got counselling; she is a strong young woman. Ann is on a methadone programme;

she attends DROP (Dún Laoghaire-Rathdown Outreach Project) in Dún Laoghaire every day and is doing well. When Ann first got counselling, I went with her. The counsellor said to me, 'You need to look after yourself and get counselling because one day you will thank your daughter.' Well, that day has come. Thank you, Ann, for giving me a voice.

ONE DAY I AM IN COLLEGE
AND THE NEXT...

Anonymous

I suppose it all began in my final year in college. I had been studying in Germany and started to feel very low and depressed towards the end of my time there. When my studies were over I decided to find a job for a few weeks before it was time to return home to college in Ireland.

I found factory work. On the first day working there I caught my hand in some machinery and had to go to hospital. I was really angry that the company had no safety precautions in place. Looking back now I believe the incident triggered off a break in my mental health. I went straight to college when I returned home from Germany. But in the end I got so bad I couldn't concentrate on any of my subjects. I made the decision to leave college. I was devastated.

I pretty much took to the bed for six months, not knowing what was wrong with me. I had always been a really strong motivated person and here I was, not even able to get out of bed. Eventually I saw a psychiatrist and was put on anti-psychotics. Although I still had very poor mental health I found work. I worked for a year and a half until I just couldn't cope any more.

Eventually the psychosis which accompanied the depression got so bad that I quit my job and put myself into the Lakeview Psychiatric Unit in Naas. I remember it being really scary. In the car with my family, on the way to the Lakeview Unit, I heard voices. They told me I would never see my family again. I was terrified.

I spent a month in the Lakeview Unit, where my medication was altered. I was diagnosed with paranoid schizophrenia and depression. I couldn't believed I had fallen from so high to so low. One minute I was a final-year university student and the next I was in a psychiatric hospital.

With the help of my family, the doctors and nurses I began to get better. The most difficult part was trying to rewire my thoughts from delusions to reality. Sometimes it was hard to distinguish between the two. I had also developed many bad habits, like napping in the middle of the day. I remember just wanting to sleep all the time. Depression brings about so much negativity in thought. I felt I had no future and lost interest in everything I used to like doing. During the healing process I began to write poetry. In the space of a month, I think I wrote almost a hundred poems. It was like a cloudburst of emotions spilling out of me. In the end the breakthrough for me was the correct medication, Clozaril. It stopped all the relapses and I haven't been back to hospital since. I would call it the wonder drug.

I went around the loop of day centres, back to wellness programmes, community employment schemes – various courses aimed to get me back to doing something positive and becoming well again. It seemed to be a never-ending circle. Then a breakthrough came when I started a full-time course in web design. I am a year and a half on this course now. I really enjoy it and it has helped me feel more confident about myself. It's now twelve years since I was diagnosed with this illness and I have been almost symptom-free for more than a year.

I also have an affordable apartment which I share with my sister, who has the same illness as me. Since then I haven't looked back. I feel positive and motivated and most of all I am again the happy person I used to be.

GROUND-HOG DAY

Bernard, Dublin

I grew up in Crumlin and got caught up with the older generation of people involved in criminality. Now when I look back and think of role models, no one ever sat me down and said, 'If you do this, *this* will happen.' I got caught up in the whole heroin scene from when I was fifteen until I was thirty-six. That drug turned me into what I would describe as a slave. Heroin came into Dublin in 1979. I took cannabis from about the age of twelve to the age of fifteen and the odd bit of LSD. Heroin was a progression from these. The first time I took it, a friend, who is dead now, said he had this new drug – Skag – and did I want to try it. Without realising it, I fell in love with it.

At twenty-one I was diagnosed with HIV. Back then I remember I was incarcerated and we would have been segregated from the main population. They brought in a professor and put a screen up and told us we would all be dead in a few years. Everything was paper cups, gloves and masks. My attitude then would have been: what's the point in stopping taking this drug. I might as well keep abusing myself.

I remember the girl I was with at the time went to the US and I went over as an illegal immigrant. I felt Dublin was the problem, my friends were the problem. But *I* was the problem and I brought the problem with me. I experienced serious withdrawals. I brought Physeptone with me and when I saw cocaine at a party I showed a lot of interest and this guy told me about Chinatown in Boston. I got heroin there and everything that happened to me in Dublin happened again in Boston. I got married and had a child.

A friend of my wife approached me at the time and asked me, 'Do you feel you have a problem?' I went into an intensive treatment programme and was living in a home with twenty lads. Advertisements about AIDS came on the television and I was listening to their reaction to the ads. I talked to a counsellor I knew who was positive as well. He encouraged me to call a group meeting to tell the others that I was HIV-positive and that I didn't like the comments they made when the ads about AIDS came on the TV. That's when I came to accept my status. I found it easy to talk to people about it after that.

I came back to Dublin in 1991 and a few years later I was using again. But it was never the same. I had a belly full of drugs but a head full of knowledge and the two didn't go together. I continued to use drugs for the next ten years. During those ten years of relapse I was clinically dead. A few of those years I spent in Mountjoy and I was dabbling in there. You'd get in with a few people who were getting drugs in on different days of the week. There were times when there were no drugs available and I'd feel the desperation and tell myself that I couldn't continue to feel like this. I'd stay in my cell for three or four days and go through the withdrawal and then someone would have drugs and I'd forget what I'd been through and use again.

In 2001 I acquired another habit – Benzos (sleeping tablets). I was on methadone, benzos, cannabis and drinking as well. I decided enough was enough and that I couldn't continue. It was groundhog day for me – every day was the same. The methadone clinic, the doctor, home. The clinic, doctor, home. I had accumulated some fines for road-traffic offences – the choice was pay €2000 or do ninety days. I would hand myself in and could detox off the methadone while incarcerated. After sixteen days in the medical wing I was told, 'Get your stuff; you're going home.' I didn't want to go and said to them, 'You're ruining what I want to do.'

My ex-wife was now living in England and she said on the phone that there was a Narcotics Anonymous conference on over there and would I think of going over? I jumped on a plane on the Saturday morning and a couple approached me at the conference and said that if I ever wanted to stop they would give me a room in their house to detox.

It felt different this time because along with everything else I was on, I was detoxing from tablets. It's not to be recommended. I was having a lot of delusions. Thoughts come rushing like a train when you stop sending up the chemicals. It was dangerous but I did come through it.

After the three weeks I left the house. There was this Dublin guy living in a recovery home and I found out I could stay there as a guest for a few days. I met this woman there from MADD (Mothers Against Drugs de Facto). I told her how I became drug-free and she couldn't believe I did it. She saw something in me. She called an emergency meeting and asked me if I would like to work there as an employee? A support worker. I worked there for a couple of years and then returned to Dublin, where I trained as a drugs worker with Addiction Response in Crumlin.

Then I went to work on a community scheme in Open Heart House, a support centre for people with HIV. When that position was coming to an end the CEO offered me a job. My role is the induction and enrollment of new members. People are vulnerable when they are first diagnosed and think they are going to die. I can share my experience with them and it is priceless to see the relief on their face. I talk them through the service and share with them my status and how long I am HIV-positive – twenty-six years now.

Inside Open Heart House I am a support worker, helping people with hospital appointments, getting a bed for the night, supporting them in whatever way we can. I am also an outreach worker on the streets and in prisons. I was seen as a hopeless case but I have come full circle.

My family is happy I have come out of it and proud that I was able to do what I have done. I am the person they phone now if there is any problem in the family whereas at one time they didn't talk to me. I enjoy my lifestyle and see it as very valuable. I live a healthy lifestyle: don't drink, smoke or take drugs. I would like to stay as healthy as I am. I like to go into a gym and work out with weights. I used to play football but I'm getting a bit old to be competing with teenagers.

I'm not willing to give up my peace of mind for any chemical. It's a great freedom.

Our Secret

Valerie Bowe

She always wanted a dog. Any dog she saw she would run over to pet, so much so that she had to be taught to ask the owner's permission first. Where animals were concerned she had no fear. I remember her daddy saying after one of the first times he brought her to the zoo that she wanted to play with the tigers! 'But I'm not afraid, Daddy,' she said. Her first pet was a goldfish, then she got a parrot and then when she was four she got a kitten. Her animal kingdom would expand as she grew older and the dog would come later when she could take more responsibility.

Conversations about getting a dog would surface from time to time and then subside. I understood the dog would be a birthday present or that Santa would bring it some year. It was during one of these intense dog conversations that I suggested to my seven-year-old granddaughter that she needed to do something about this dream she had. She needed to fast-forward it, so to speak. What could she do?

I suggested we snuggle up on the bed together and have a look at the DVD of the book, *The Secret*. There is a little boy in it who desperately wants a bike – but it is not happening. It is explained that the boy has to do three things – two of which he had done. The third thing he had to do was to imagine he has the bike. This he starts to do. He psyches himself up – drawing the bike, feeling he has the bike, riding the bike. Then he gets the bike!

So, Saoirse, I said, you've got to do the same. What kind of a dog would you like? She said it was a choice between two. But which one do you want? I really want a King Charles spaniel, she said. I explained to her that she had to be clear about what she wanted as it wouldn't work if she was undecided. Okay, a King Charles spaniel was what she really wanted. Now, what is the dog's name? Rosie if it's a girl and Diamond if it's a boy. What is the dog doing? He is licking my face. What else? He is jumping up on my bed? I am taking him for a walk. And? I am cleaning up his poo! Wow!

Now I suggested that she start to buy little things for the dog in the pet shop. I would help her and start it off. I would buy her one of those ball-fetchers for when she brought the dog out for a walk.

Saoirse's anticipation and excitement about getting this dog rose and rose. I was beginning to be a little worried that I might be overstepping my role as a granny but I persisted. We had a great laugh and really got into the spirit of the thing, so much so that at one point Saoirse, with a great big grin on her face, pointed to the end of the bed and said, 'Appear, dog, now!'

The next evening she phoned me, very excited, and said, 'You know Nana Val, the imagination thing we were doing?' She must have been to the pet shop and bought a dog toy, I thought.

'Oh, you mean the Secret?' I said. 'Yeah, yeah.'

She was getting more and more excited. 'Well, I have the dog!' '

'What?'

'I got the dog,' she said.

I caught myself in a moment of disbelief. Hold on now. 'You have the dog, a King Charles spaniel?'

'Yes, yes,' she said.

In twenty-four hours she had it.

After school the next day her mammy brought Saoirse on a drive and when Saoirse said, 'I'm bored, Where are we going?' she told her, 'We're going to Wexford to get a dog.'

'I cried when my mammy told me,' Saoirse said

later as she told me the whole story in detail. 'I wasn't really crying,' she added. 'I cried because I was so delighted.'

Rites of Passage

Dave Fennell, County Meath

It was the summer of 2008 and that March my son Conor had celebrated his twelfth birthday. I had been doing a range of work on myself and was reading up on different ethnic groups and tribal people, particularly from South America and South Africa. I learned that it is standard among indigenous people to hold initiation ceremonies when a boy is changing into manhood.

The only initiation I could see in Ireland was in the form of taking your son for a pint, or maybe boys amongst themselves, trying to fit in, daring one another to steal something or rob an orchard. These were examples but they weren't very positive.

I was very struck that at the age of twelve, in places like Kenya, a young boy is brought into scrub/jungle and literally walked into manhood, while being supported by his elders. The child is assisted in facing his fears. That's where the idea came from: to challenge my son to face his fears while I supported him.

Looking back on our Celtic roots we don't have the tradition of the jungle but we have the countryside and I thought: what are the elements we *do* have? Water is one. So we went camping to a remote campsite near a lake in County Cavan. Packed up the car but kept things simple too. Lake water is dark and dense and quite scary but when you get into it it is a lovely feeling.

The initiation would comprise three tasks. The first night two could be completed. The tasks had to be achievable yet challenging.

When Conor saw the lake, he nearly died. It took him quite a while to come around to the idea of getting in. I told him it was about facing his fears and standing on his own, that I was there to support him but I couldn't help him. I kept reassuring him and eventually he got in and swam in the dark, dense lake. The fear on his face was palpable. He came out and the adrenaline was pumping; he was exhilarated. He was running up and down, delighted with himself. I said, 'Well done.'

The next task was to climb something. There was a huge old tree nearby. I was good at climbing myself and was able to pass on a few skills to him. 'I can't do that,' he said. I showed him a few things to look out for and told him to use his head and his initiative.

'I can see for miles,' he yelled when he got up to the top. 'But how do I get down?'

That night we cooked and lit a candle and he was buzzing. 'What is the next task?' he asked. 'Will I be able for it?'

The initiation ceremonies in other cultures always included a wild animal so in an Irish context, what would the equivalent be?

I had to be mindful of a number of things, like trespassing and bulls in fields. We drove around for some time until we came across a gully and beyond there were cows with their calves. 'No way, I can't do this,' he said. I talked to him and encouraged him to try. At one point I was not sure if he would do it or not but I kept encouraging him. He was really nervous. He had to walk through the animals and touch a cow but he did it.

I said to my son, 'No matter what comes at you in life I want you to think of this day.'

I congratulated Conor on his courage and told him he had completed his initiation. Then we had our own celebration.

ONE OF THE RICHEST
COUNTRIES IN THE WORLD

Mohanad, an Iraqi Citizen Living in Dublin

My family used to live a very quiet and lovely life. I am an engineer and could provide for all the family's needs and buy a fancy house, as well as establishing a specialised manufacturing workshop and an engineering services office in centre of Baghdad. I had a healthy bank account. We had close connections with all our relatives (a big family of ten brothers and two sisters, all married). I used to take care of the needs of my extended family as well; I paid for the marriage of my younger brother, took care of the medical needs of my elderly parents and so on.

After the invasion in 2003, I started working on a report for a prestigious news agency, in my capacity as a mechanical engineer, regarding the WMDs (weapons of mass destruction) that Saddam was supposed to have.

Things started to change; suddenly and unexpectedly. Some people were very happy to get rid of the Saddam regime and believed that the country was finally free. For a rich country like Iraq, people believed that things could change in a short space of time. But the reality was totally different, for many reasons: the dishonesty of the invaders, the followers of the defeated regime and so on. By mid- to late-2005, Iraqi people were disappointed by the lack of general services and the lack of security. Very soon the civil and sectarian war started, with everyone exposed to grave danger for no reason at all. You had to take care of everything for yourself: find your own way to get electricity, food, medicine and finance and to protect your family.

In mid-April 2006, my cousin, who was a technician working for an electricity distribution company, was killed at work for unknown reasons. Exactly two weeks later, my brother-in-law (my wife's twin brother), who was a surgeon, was shot on his way home from work and left to die. These were two great shocks for the whole family and left us wondering: who's next and when.

Then every family got a death threat to move immediately from their houses, leaving all their belongings inside. Sunnis had to leave and go to Sunni areas and the same for the Shiites. But it's a bit complicated in my family. We are ten brothers and have a Sunni father and a Shiite mother, I myself am a Sunni but I am married to my cousin on my mother's side so, my wife is a Shiite. It's the same for most of my brothers, who are Sunnis, married to Shiite women.

We left our houses empty and rented new houses in different areas. Every night when we went to bed, I would lock all doors with metal bars and put a gun under my pillow. My daughter Sarah, born two and a half years after the invasion, reminded me one night to bring the gun. That cut me deep inside as I wanted my kids to be reared in a better way, especially as I had not owned any kind of weapons in my life, not even a knife.

I told my wife if we got attacked by militia at night to hide with the kids in our secret shelter under the steps and not to make any noise even if they killed me in order to save herself and the children.

At the end of 2006, the press agency I used to work for in Baghdad published a story about the worst militia in Iraq, which was supported by the Iranian and Iraqi governments and was responsible for the kidnapping and assassination of foreigners and Iraqi civilians. As the office manager of this agency I helped to arrange and carry out interviews for this story.

This put me in a critical situation, with my family facing a threat of death. In August 2006 my twenty-five-year-old nephew was killed and two weeks later, a cousin and his wife were killed. They were both engineers. After this assassination, I decided to leave Iraq and look for a safe place to live.

In January 2007, a gang of insurgents belonging, I believe, to Mehdi militia, chased me in the centre of Baghdad. They pointed at me with their weapons, signalling me to stop. That's what they usually do, kidnap, torture, then kill their hostages (Sunni people and those who work for the Americans and British). I survived by the help of God: I found an army checkpoint so I stopped next to them and pretended that my car was broken down. I was really terrified. I moved with my family to a relative's house and never went to work again.

My elder son's name is Omar, a very clear Sunni name: having a name like this is enough to get you killed. I changed his name from Omar to Mohammed because the militias were chasing people who had this name.

Before I left Iraq, I settled my family in my wife's parents' house. They live in a Shiite area and the militia won't be looking for Sunnies there; besides, my wife is a Shiite and living with her Shiite parents. It was risky but I had no other choice: at least my father and brothers-in-law can defend my family and say that they are Shiite. We told our kids to call Omar nothing but Mohammed.

I was lucky to come to Ireland seeking asylum in February 2007. My status was approved as a recognised refugee in July 2007. They were vulnerable, devastating months I spent, worried about the children and my wife, having left them in danger back in Iraq. But I was pretty sure that it was my turn to be killed next and thought it worthwhile to suffer for a few months in order to find peace.

Thank God, Irish people were very kind and generous and understanding of my situation. Finally my family reunification was approved in June 2008 and we were all reunited fourteen months later. We spent the interim chatting via Skype and Yahoo Messenger. I was watching Sarah's hair growing every time we chatted. She was so proud of it and always asking when we would see each other again.

Sarah is now in school in Dublin and doing very well: her teacher says that she is the best student in her class.

My wife and I are so happy and grateful that we and our four children can finally live in a safe shelter where humanity is appreciated and my children can live their life like children anywhere in the world. They get their education, use computers, make new friends and have teachers they can trust.

Azuz, my ten-year-old, is a lovely boy and crazy about soccer. He is now in fifth class here in Dublin and doing very well in his class. He has lots of loving friends and, most important for him, he's playing a lot of soccer.

The whole family is recovering from the old suffering and trying to integrate with the Irish community. Since the day I arrived, I have been attending English courses to improve my English. I also did a computer course in a college in Dublin and took on some voluntary work as an IT teacher for a few months. The recession and the job situation are affecting everybody but we hope things will get better very soon.

It is so sad that things are still bad in Iraq. Although it is a very rich country the war has destroyed everything, not just the infrastructure but even the life of the people as regards security, education and medical care.

At this time, we feel lucky to be in Ireland and are really sorry about the situation in our home country.

In My Heart I Knew

Ann Hughes, Tullamore

She was born into a family of boys. The first year of Debbie's life was no different from my other children. I became anxious as little things began to worry me about her behaviour: not responding; screaming rather than trying to talk when she wanted to make a point or get her own way. Aggression, trying to pull long hair if she could get it, also someone's glasses – and it was always done with speed.

In my heart I knew something was strange, but it was like if I didn't talk about it, even to my husband Paul, it would go away.

At a family christening, it was looking me in the face. I broke down and sobbed. I felt that the members of my family, which was a big family, all knew but did not like to say anything.

When I calmed down, Paul and I agreed that I should go to the family doctor the following day. My worries were confirmed. Debbie was in a world of her own, not responding to anything around her except to certain voices that caused her to scream.

Consultant Professor Conor Ward worked in Crumlin but came to Navan, where we lived, once a month. He saw Deb. He did tests and she failed miserably. My heart was broken. His words were, 'She will not go to a normal school, play with toys or other children. She will go to a special school as she is mentally handicapped.' I can still picture that moment: his words, his face, his kindness, which comforted. It stays with you all your life; it's like a scar inside.

We went to Dublin to tell Mam and Dad. All poor Mam could do was pour a few brandies into me but there was no relief from the pain. As time went on, I cried for every little girl I saw because Deb could not be like them. She looked beautiful but it was as if inside there was a little monster. Anything she could reach, she wrecked. My whole family and my boys' lives were turned upside down, big time. Paul took time off work to try to help me. We were a handicapped family: husband, wife and siblings.

When she was three, we brought Deb to see Professor Paul McQuaid in Morehampton Road in Dublin. He said she was autistic and he would like her to go to St Michael's House in Dublin but as we were living in Navan, that was not on the cards. My next move was to talk to Father Andy Farrell in Navan. We had a lovely day-care centre built for children like Deb. Some were worse than her, some not as bad, and the staff were great. Father Farrell got her in there when she was three. There she could be showered, bathed and potty-trained if possible. From that year on, Debs spread faeces on herself: on walls, anywhere she could reach, so that often, you could see only her little eyes. What a life! There were times I wanted to walk away, as this was beyond what anyone could cope with. But she was my child. I loved her and hated her. My boys cried out for attention but Deb got attention no matter what. I was so bitter. My only girl was beautiful but in a different world I and my husband and boys did not understand.

Deb made her First Communion in a classroom. Most normal places frightened her so Sister Saviour arranged a room with an altar, a lovely priest, her family and her little friends. She cried the whole way through with fear. Again she looked beautiful. To see someone so distressed and not know what makes them so frightened or how to comfort them or is awful but this has been the way for most of Deb's life.

I cannot go into every detail of Deb's life as it would go on for ever so I will highlight some good times. Deb can be funny in a very natural way. She is also affectionate on her terms. If she is really excited over something she runs to you, hands out to hug. It is seldom you will get eye contact. She used to rock on her bed but stopped about five years ago. Another thing that gave her comfort was a swing: she would stay on a swing for hours with her headset on, listening to music. She was in her own little world, with no fear, happy.

Deb never had friends so it's a lonely life for her but my friends are all very good to her and she is included in everything. One of my friends has a son who is autistic. He is twenty and a beautiful gentle boy and she calls him her boyfriend. For them to meet up, his mam and I must make the arrangements. To us their get-togethers are worth it: they are both autistic but they are very different.

Deb has been in different schools that did not work out. We had to fight for every service and then take what was available. Thank God I was able to do this for Deb and I will continue to do it for as long as I am able. Growing up we were always taught that children like Deb were God's special children but it is clear that the government does not think like that. As a mother your life is hard enough without fighting with the HSE for every little bit of help you need.

I talk about Deb as if she was still a child but she is thirty-one now: she has the body of a woman but is a child inside, all excited about toy shops and Christmas, also loving style, make-up and bling, like any young person. Deb is in the best place of her life at the moment: she goes to a day centre with great staff and has a few nights' respite to give her a break from home, which also gives me a break. When Deb is happy I am happy. People often ask me, 'How do you do it?' and my answer is, 'For the love of Deb.' There is not a night before I go to sleep that I do not ask God to spare me for as long as possible. We are joined at the hip and it breaks my heart to think what will happen to her when I am gone.

I have been a member of the Carers' Association in Tullamore for eight years and I love our support-group meetings. We all have different issues and when we get together we feel better for realising we're not on our own. I'm not a bit shy and often get up and talk in public about my experience, for instance at the Carers' Association pre-budget launch in Buswell's Hotel and recently at an event in the Mansion House. People came up to me and said I spoke from the heart and that I was easier to understand than someone rattling on about something. I feel, no matter what problem comes at me, I've been there, done that.

Living to a Hundred and Four

Nicola, Dublin

I am a thirty-six-year-old women living in the suburbs of Dublin. When I was eighteen I did voluntary work for Body Positive on National AIDS Awareness Days, selling red ribbons and giving out free condoms. That is where I met my partner and discovered he was HIV-positive. We had an on-off relationship for about a year and a half. During this time he often asked me why it didn't bother me that he had HIV but to be honest I was eighteen and in love and wasn't looking to the future.

When we were on one of our breaks I had a brief fling with a bloke I knew a long time. This was when I decided to go for my first test because if I had it I didn't want to pass it on to him. Thank God it was negative.

My partner and I had been back together for a few months when I realised I was pregnant so I had a sense then that I was positive but I didn't want to believe it.

He and I split up soon after and my ma came with me for the results. When the doctor said I was positive my poor ma was devastated. She asked, 'How long has she got?' The doctor told her that people were living longer with it all the time. While I was pregnant, I was asked to take a drug called AZT, to stop transmission of the virus from mother to baby. It was only on trial at the time but I took it because I thought even if it didn't help me it might help the next person.

I was about eight months pregnant when my ma was diagnosed with bone cancer. We were told that she could live fifteen to twenty years but sadly she passed away when my son was six weeks old. I don't remember much about the next year as I felt as if I was in a bubble and this wasn't my life. It was as if I was looking in on someone else's life.

I had to bring my son for regular check-ups for the virus until he was eighteen months old. Every time he was sick, even if he had a cold, I would think, 'What have I done?' I thank God every day that he is negative and now he is nearly fifteen.

We have a great relationship. I think that is because there have only been the two of us: I haven't been in a relationship since he was three years old. This has been my choice as I wanted to rear him by myself.

My family was very supportive and helped me

out a lot. I can talk to my sisters so I am not holding things in. We are a lot closer now that we are older and all live in close range of one another.

It was only this year that I started thinking about my HIV again – why, I don't know. Maybe because my son is older now so he doesn't need me as much and I've more time on my hands as I am unemployed at the moment. This is hard as I've always worked.

I have always considered that I don't live with HIV – it lives with me – and I have never been sick from it. I do take tablets every day and will for the rest of my life. Sometimes it gets to me but then I remember what my ma always said, 'No matter how bad you think your life is, there is always someone worse off than you,' and I pick myself up because that's what she would want me to do.

I started going to a place called Open Heart House, a support network for people living with HIV and AIDS and I have to say it is a great place. I also volunteer in there once a week. The people are lovely and from all walks of life. It has really helped me and I've come so far since going in there that it's giving me more confidence in myself.

I still have to tell my son about my HIV. I didn't tell him before as I think kids should be kids and not have to worry about things like this. But he is not a child any more. He will be okay as he is a great kid and we have a great relationship,

We are all going to die some day. My time is not up yet. My granny was a hundred and three when she died and I'll be a hundred and four.

A Small Farm
in Ballymote

Mary Davey, Sligo

I grew up on a small farm in the townland of Roskeymore, Cuffada, County Sligo. I was born in March 1918, the second-eldest of four children to Margaret and John Kielty. Cuffada was a tiny village with a shop, school and church.

I met my future husband Patrick (pet-name Bab) at a gathering around a bonfire when I was fourteen or fifteen years old. He was from the adjoining parish of Knockbruck and one of nine children. We got married in 1945 when I was twenty-seven and Bab was forty. We had eight children: five girls and three boys. At the start of our married life together we bought a small farm in Ballymote, a town seven miles from my townland, Cuffada.

As well as farming, Bab worked as a carpenter and his craftsmanship was much sought-after but the land always remained a great source of pride for us both. The turf was cut to heat our home for the winter. The cows, calves, sheep, pigs and poultry ensured good nutrition for the family. Our extensive vegetable garden meant food all year round and in a good year the excess vegetables, milk, eggs and turf meant 'pocket money' for the children and me.

In the early 1970s, I noticed that Bab began yo lose things, occasionally forgetting where he had left familiar items. We always ate our lunch at 1.30 while listening to the news on the radio. One of the first changes in this routine happened when I visited Chicago for my grandson's christening and my daughter Maria came home to Ballymote to be with Bab. He arrived in from the farm at eleven o'clock looking for lunch. Maria told him it was too early but he proceeded to check out the cooker and saucepans. Isolated incidents like this soon became a pattern and it became apparent that Bab had a major memory problem.

Every day brought its own difficulty. I met Bab in town wearing only one shoe. His usual cigarette purchase of one packet of ten or twenty weekly increased to several packets. Always a cautious man with money and alcohol, he would now sell cattle more frequently, not bank the money and on his once-a-week trip to the pub he would treat others to a round. The owner (Des Kielty, a relative) brought this to my notice. Bab would make the trip to town several times during day and evening, neglecting his beloved gardening and farming tasks.

The only things that made it tolerable for me were Bab's calmness and easy personality and mostly he listened to my advice in those early years. My lifeline was phone contact with the children and we frequently went to Dublin to visit them. On one such trip, when we were returning home to Ballymote by train, Bab went to the toilet, missed his stop and ended up in Sligo. One of our wonderful friends and neighbour, John McNulty (RIP) drove to Sligo to try and find him but was unsuccessful. This was a very frightening and distressing episode. Thank God he arrived safely home at lunchtime the following day – to this day I will never know how he made it home.

The family came together and made the decision that it was no longer possible for me to care for Bab at home on my own. By the early 1980s we made the decision to move to Dublin and live with our children, who helped enormously to ease the burden for me. This was a very big upheaval in Bab's and my way of life: leaving behind the countryside, our farming life and our great neighbours, family and friends. However, for Bab's safety and my peace of mind, I knew it had to be done.

Life was very different in Dublin but I made the adjustment. I recall a few very stressful instances when Bab managed to leave the house quietly (despite a lot of attention to his security) and went missing for a period of time – one in particular.

He managed to remove the lock from the door and slip out into the busy street. He passed the American Embassy and crossed the railway line into Sandymount. This happened at around eight in the evening on a very cold rugby weekend in March. I will never forget our distress as we prayed and searched for him. We were very fortunate that the local Gardai coordinated the search with us. Eight hours later we found Bab safe and happy, enjoying the company and post-match celebrations with a wonderful family in Sandymount. He had knocked on their door, cold, hungry and tired. The door was opened by a Mr Carty, a local solicitor, who recognised Bab's symptoms from his father-in-law who had suffered from dementia. They kindly took him in and he joined in their food and festivities.

Many hours later we got the call to say that Bab was with them, safe and well. He had listed many names and addresses from the past, to no avail, when he eventually remembered the twenty-four-hour shop in Rathmines (a family business). Maria and Phil went to collect him and found him merrily singing and full of praise for these wonderful people. That episode will never leave my mind, especially the kindness of that family and everyone involved in his safe return.

I managed to attend the local church organisation in Ballsbridge, which was a welcome outlet for me. Fortunately we had no further major scares and Bab was lovingly cared for until his death on 18 March 1984.

After Bab's death I returned to Ballymote, hoping to settle back into my old way of life, but I found it very lonely without him. I kept remembering the way life was before Bab's illness and the happy years we spent working and rearing our family. After a few months I came to the realisation that I would never settle down there on my own and with the family's encouragement I came to live in Maynooth, County Kildare in the house of my daughter, Bernadette, as she was living abroad.

This was a very positive move, helped enormously by the kindness and support of three wonderful families – the Smiths, Hogans and Martins. Sheila Smith suggested that I take in students and it gave me a daily focus and secured my financial independence. Many of the students and their families have remained great friends. In the 1980s I suffered the near fatal effects of a long-term heart condition but thanks to my doctor and geriatrician and my daughter Cathy, who is a nurse, I am well cared for. In 2001 I moved not too far away to live with my daughter Maria, son-in-law John and granddaughter, Michala. Now in my ninety-third year, I close my eyes each night, saying a lovely prayer my grandfather taught me, 'Night Has Fallen', and thanking God for my wonderful family and friends. I feel ready for His final call.

IRELAND'S FIRST

Tara Leech, Dublin

I am a gymnast. My routines are high beam, floor, vault and high bars. Three years ago I developed a hip problem and had to have an operation in Cappagh Hospital. I'm no longer able to do gymnastics but I trained to be an assistant coach. I was a member of Bayside Gymnastics Club and Marie Carroll was my coach when I was competing. I work with Marie now as an assistant coach.

I had to do my training through the British Gymnastics Federation to become an accredited gym coach for special needs. My training included first aid; how to care for the equipment in the gym; helping athletes with their postures and awareness of some sports injuries. I like doing massage and I am now thinking about doing a course in sports massage.

In 2003, in Croke Park, I became a gold medallist at the Special Olympics. I also received overall Gymnast of the Year award.

I did my Leaving Certificate in St Tiernan's Community School in Dundrum. After that I received my certificate in pre-school play groups and worked in childcare for a number of years. Then I went to work for my brother in catering. I have also worked in the Michelin-starred restaurant, Chapter One. I hold a certificate in advocacy from UCD and DCU. At the moment I am doing my final paper for a special needs' assistant's course and then I will be Ireland's first special needs' assistant with Down's Syndrome. I was born with Down's Syndrome. It is just something I have. I have to listen a bit harder than other people so I can understand – but I am a good listener.

I come from a big family and have four brothers and two sisters. They think Down's Syndrome makes me special. Everyone needs help and support whether they have a disability or not. To help others I became an ambassador for the Down's Syndrome Association and represented Ireland at the first International Synod of People with Down's Syndrome and at the EU Day of Disability Council in Brussels in 2009.

My other sports are swimming and golf. My biggest dream now is to become a swimmer like my friend David and compete in the Special Olympic World Games in the future.

Believe in God
and Believe in Yourself

Majella Reid, County Mayo

Although it happened less than two years ago, it is sometimes hard to remember the darkest hours of my soul. As I sit here in my sitting room surrounded by tealights and mellow music, with my puppy playing at my feet, I find it difficult to relive the endless nights with no light at the end of the tunnel.

It is now eighteen months since my psychiatrist, Dr Murphy, diagnosed me as having bipolar disorder. I sat in the small yellow room in St Loman's Hospital, Mullingar, waiting as she browsed through her thick manila folder. I no longer cared what she was going to say. For me, it was all a nightmare. It was my third admission in six months and over a period of two years I had lost everything: a marriage, a home, a business, friendships and, of course, I had repeatedly lost my mind.

This was my greatest loss and certainly my greatest humiliation. I have a bachelor's degree in journalism and a masters in business administration. I was not the type of woman who ended up in and out of psychiatric hospital, yet here I was – a woman whose mind was seriously ill.

'How do you feel about your diagnosis?' asked Dr Murphy.

What could I say? I didn't know what bipolar disorder (BP) was. I was sick of hospital, medication, psychiatric terminology. I was later to learn that BP is a mental condition whereby my mind (without medication) can move from states of mania (elation) to periods of deep depression.

I was no stranger to these moods. During one period of elation I had gone missing in London for more than forty-eight hours, only to be found in the psychiatric ward of a hospital in west London. This was my first nervous breakdown and perhaps the worst.

The depression was equally horrific: a dragging weariness and lack of energy. Suicidal thoughts were common and although I never attempted to take my own life, I was sorely tempted.

So what carried me through to this lighter time in my life? An accident. Some days after I was diagnosed with BP I was put on a medication that did not agree with me. The result was that I collapsed in a shower, banging my head on the ground, and was consequently rushed to Mullingar General Hospital. I felt shame at being in a 'normal' hospital. Shame that the staff and those around me would know that I was from St Loman's. That I was a 'loony'.

A doctor from Iraq, whose name I do not know, asked me about myself and when I did not answer readily he smiled down at me and said, 'Believe in God and believe in yourself.'

That was the beginning of my recovery. Repeatedly over the days, weeks and months that followed, I reminded myself of his words. I believe in God and I believe in that part of me that is connected to God, my soul.

I know that my soul is here to experience and grow in this lifetime and I will never give up on it. As long as I believe in God and believe in myself I know that I can not only make it through but I can reach – have reached – a place where life is worth living again.

Let Me Back to My JCB

Andy McGovern, County Leitrim

I was born in 1933, on a small farm in Corroneary, Aughavas, in south Leitrim, The most important thing in my life, I was told, was to be a good strong workman, not a pen-pushing, muscle-starved, useless 'get'. To be a good ploughman, a good turf-cutter, a good haymaker eventually would secure my destiny. I grew up strong. At the age of twenty, I had mastered most important jobs on our thirty-acre farm, only to discover that these back-breaking tasks yielded very little financial return.

In 1953, I emigrated to London and became a barman, a change from the plough, loy or turf-spade. It was not long before I moved to construction work, to make plenty of money. Each year, I would return to help at peak periods on the farm. In 1961, I got married and in 1962 our first child was born, a son. We decided to return to Ireland and bring up our children the Irish way. In 1964 we returned to County

Leitrim and, ironically, set up on a small farm. I got a job as a lorry driver, to help subsidise our low income. Later, I bought an excavator, a JCB (with the help of a loan), the first of its kind in the district. Now I was self-employed, my own boss! But, as I was soon to find out, it is really hard work toiling for oneself. I worked that machine night and day until I nearly fell off it.

One day in 1976, I noticed my right arm was a bit weak. Months later, while extending this arm, I saw one finger dropping, unable to resist the pull of gravity. Not to worry. Were there not nine more to go? In 1977, another finger fell and it was time to act.

I went to my doctor, who found nothing wrong, although he suspected a nerve problem. He warned me that, although the condition might be arrested, there would be no reversing a damaged nerve.

After numerous tests and long periods in a Dublin hospital, finally, in 1978, I was diagnosed as having a terminal illness known as motor neurone disease (MND). So far, medical research has failed to find a cause or a cure. A simple explanation of what happens is that the message from brain to muscle somehow becomes interrupted, causing the neurones to die, resulting in massive muscle-wasting in the part of the body affected.

The disease is not confined to any one part of the body. As the years pass, it attacks other areas, such as neck, throat, speech organs, lungs and breathing equipment, eventually resulting in death, usually from respiratory failure. Life expectancy with this disease is between two and five years, according to the experts.

You can well imagine my anxiety and frustration when a neurologist at St Vincent's Hospital, Dublin, diagnosed this fatal disease. Then aged forty-five, I was absolutely devastated. With a wife and six children, aged from sixteen down to three, this was not the future I had anticipated. I continued to work as an excavator driver, though with limited power in one arm. Looking back, I could say that I was on the first rung of the ladder to success.

In 1980, with my arm somewhat weaker, I decided to go to Lourdes. I stared straight in the face at the statue of our Blessed Lady. I said, 'Cure me and let me back to my JCB.'

At the end of that 1980 pilgrimage a Madame director gave our group a lecture, telling us something of the few miracles that had happened in Lourdes. She said that all those who came to Lourdes receive some gift: 'It may happen while you are in Lourdes. It may happen when you return home, or in years to come.

But, eventually, everyone will receive something.' I returned home from that pilgrimage a happy man. I would not have long to wait for my gift. Had I not put in the 'twist', as far as prayer and devotion were concerned.

One, two, three years on and my arm got weaker and weaker. I started using my left arm and hand for every little chore. By four or five years later, the condition had spread to my left arm. I became bitter, infuriated and angry, angry with God, angry with the whole religious concept.

'Why me?' I shouted. I had kept my end of the bargain and had received nothing. Seven, eight, nine years, and everything that I touched fell to the ground.

Then one day in May 1990 two women visited me. They were from CASA (Caring and Sharing Association). It was obvious that they knew all about my disease. They invited me to visit Lourdes with their association the following July. 'Lourdes!' I said, trying hard to control my rage and not to offend them. 'I went to Lourdes ten years ago and got nothing!'

One of the visitors, a nun, Sister Mary, said, 'Andy, not many people live ten years with that disease. What do you mean, you got nothing? Physically, you look great to me.'

They would allocate a good carer to me, they

promised. And they did. Some 30,000 feet over the mountains, I was introduced to my carer, a young, energetic, athletic, Corkman twenty years my junior. We hit it off right away. At least we had one thing in common, the same Christian name, Andrew. Next morning, he had me out of bed, shaved, showered and 'shammied' in fifteen minutes flat.

That pilgrimage went like a dream. I found myself totally relaxed, not praying for anything in particular, just going with the flow. Then, one night, nearing the end of this great tour, our group visited the grotto at midnight. My carer and I were the last of our group walking around. He rubbed my useless hands against the glazed rock and prayed. The tranquillity and quietness of this holy place was awesome: just the birds chirping in the ivy over the grotto; the sound of traffic in the distance; hundreds of people of all nationalities moving slowly, as if in a daze. This must surely be heaven on earth, I thought: just let it be.

We lit candles and drank water from the taps, still in prayer. When we came back to reality we looked around and discovered that our group had returned to the hotel. My carer whispered in my ear, 'We will have to get a move on.'

He took off in strides not recommended for the weak-hearted. I matched him every step of the way, with great effort. As we approached the main road, we could see the emblem of our association (blue headgear) stepping on to the footpath on the far side of the road. The traffic started moving, leaving us on the kerb. I was glad of this for it gave me time to draw my breath. I looked sideways at my carer, who had his hand up to his face, trying to control his laughter.

'What are you laughing at?' I asked quietly.

He turned towards me, now a bit more serious, and said, 'Ah, sure, you're the fittest invalid in Lourdes.'

The traffic stopped. We crossed the road and were soon reunited with our group.

That night, I lay awake in bed for some time, thinking about that remark, 'You're the fittest invalid in Lourdes.' To me it was not funny. Nobody had ever told me that I was an invalid and I had probably been avoiding this stigmatising term all those years.

Next morning, the final day of that 1990 pilgrimage, we visited the grotto for the last time. As we waited our turn, ironically I found myself kneeling on the very same spot where I had knelt ten years previously. I looked up at the statue of Our Lady of Lourdes. I felt guilt, shame and remorse. How could I have been so stupid, so demanding, so selfish, seeing nobody sick except myself? All those years, torturing myself with the 'why me' syndrome. In fact, I had received the greatest gift given to anybody: acceptance. For ten long years I had suffered hell because I failed to recognise that gift.

Today, physically, I'm worse off but inside I'm a happier and more contented person.

High-tech equipment was supplied to me by the Irish Motor Neurone Disease Association, of which I have been a member since its foundation in 1985. Fourteen years ago, they delivered a computer and printer to my home, showed me how to write my name (Andy), left me three instruction manuals and said, 'Goodbye.' Can you imagine a man sitting in front of a computer for the first time, with nothing but his right foot to make it work? You can well imagine my anxiety and frustration when a staff nurse, Mary Mulligan, and an occupational therapist, Nuala Tierney, at Our Lady of Lourdes Hospital, Dún Laoghaire, suggested that I write a book. My immediate reply was; 'When will pigs fly?'

But they insisted. 'You definitely have the material, if you could get it down on paper.' I persevered, making hundreds of mistakes. But, as the man said, there's only one failure in life, the failure to learn from failure. They transformed a disability into 'this' ability by encouraging me to search for the power within. My book was called, *They Laughed at this Man's Funeral.*

In 1998, I went on local radio to highlight awareness of MND. At first I was nervous. The interviewer
questioned me in detail about the disease. Soon I
regained my confidence: I knew more about this
illness than he did! That interview went splendidly.

'Are you doing anything for the association?' he
asked. I said I intended to climb Croagh Patrick on
Sunday, 13 July 1998, to raise funds for the association
and if there was anybody out there who would like to
sponsor me, I would be grateful for the support.

When I came off air, the phone started ringing
with offers of help, support and funds. The local
newspapers, *The Leitrim Observer* and *The Longford
Leader*, published articles about my expedition.
Encouraging letters and funds arrived from many
places. People with whom I had lost touch contacted
me after a silence of forty years.

The mountain looked huge in the distance. The
first stage of the climb was not too bad. We rested; I
looked up; the peak was half a mile up. I'll never make
it, I said to myself. Then we started climbing again
and I searched for the hero inside me. He responded!

I feel very privileged to have survived more than
thirty-three years with this disease. I am Ireland's
longest survivor with MND. Most patients are not so
lucky.

There is a special place on our farm for which I head each day. It is a quiet, derelict spot with a bush, a shrub, rock and some fern. It is of no agricultural value whatsoever. Nobody else comes here. The only visitors are from the wild. There I sit for about ten minutes in total solitude, weather permitting, taking in good, fresh, clean, blue air, absorbing the tranquillity of this isolated place. I close my eyes and try to cut off everything. The birds sing in the trees nearby; an ass brays far away – a sound fast becoming obsolete. Hens cackle at a neighbour's house and a cock replies to a rival. Everything here is perfect! If I were to die in this place, nobody would find me for hours, perhaps days. A frightening thought, you might say, but the solace of being alone in this timeless place far outweighs any such fear. This is heaven, my heaven.

My main wish today is to share myself with other people, now that the gift of acceptance has changed my life for ever. 'If you can break the chains on your mind you can break the chains on your body too.' I don't know what the future holds but I face my future in the knowledge that God will give me the strength to deal with whatever comes my way.

'THE HOUSE BELONGS TO ME.'

Anonymous

We were upstairs in our new house when suddenly she dragged me by the scruff of the neck into the office and pushed me down on the office table. 'The house belongs to me,' she said. She managed the money. She was an accountant. When she was calmer I talked to her and she said once I earned more money I could look after the finances.

I said to her mother that she had a bit of a temper. Her mother agreed and said she had told the doctor about this when she was a child and he said to put her out the back until she calmed down.

Before this incident my girlfriend was prone to bouts of anger but never violence. We got married and had a honeymoon baby. When she was pregnant she wouldn't let me out of her sight. The anger resurfaced. One day she came at me, punching me in the hall. I ran out the front door. She started to scream at me and stood on an upstairs window sill, threatening to throw herself off. Again I talked to her mother and asked her what I should do? She said to walk away. I asked my wife why she was doing this and she said she just wanted to hurt me the way I was hurting her by walking away.

The violent outbursts became a habit and then 'normal' behaviour. I began to accept them as part of our relationship. We were living in the country and I thought it would be a good idea to move into town and nearer to her mother.

After the birth of our first child her mother asked me a strange question. Would you not get a vasectomy? What? My wife denied discussing this with her mother. She cried when she found out she was pregnant on our second child. Things got worse and there were various incidents.

In the kitchen one morning, she had the child in her arms and was screaming. She put the child down on the table and she kept screaming, 'Don't hit me. I've never raised a hand to you.' She then sank her teeth into me – through a leather jacket.

I went to the hospital and it was the first time that I came out with it. I cried. The doctor wrote a report. Prior to this I had said nothing to my family. I thought I'd deal with it myself and be a man about it. I told my dad I couldn't manage her. He said he knew there was

something wrong. He suggested I go to Accord and
said they had trained counsellors there. I asked what I
could do in the interim. He said to move out. I spoke
to my wife and I decided to stay in the house until we
got marriage counselling. After three days she agreed.

At the first session I mentioned the violence and
she walked out. I had to apologise to her. At the
second session I mentioned money: her salary was
going into an account that I didn't even know existed.
She had been telling people we were living on one
salary. She said I was accusing her of robbing money.
We cancelled the third session as we were getting on
well. The counsellor had to cancel the fourth and
by the time the fifth appointment came around she
had convinced me that we had resolved everything. I
reluctantly agreed to cancel altogether.

I lost my job and the anger flared up again. Her
mother asked me how I could live like this and would
we not be better off separating. Her uncle was also in
the house at the time. My jaw dropped as there had
never been any question of that. I asked my wife if
this was what she wanted. Yeah, she said.

I asked her mother and her uncle to leave so that
we could discuss the situation. They refused at first
but eventually they left.

I agreed to move back to the house we had left

in the country and my spirits rose at the thought of leaving but my brother warned me that if I left she could say I had abandoned the family. I had no experience of separation either from family or friends. My sister was concerned for the kids. I began to have my doubts and decided to stay.

My brother advised me to get on the Internet and see if there was a self-help group for people in my situation. I found AMEN. They assured me that no incident of violence in a home is tolerated by law and, like my brother, advised me not to leave the house. So I applied for a protection order. The judge heard it that day. I was scared that when my wife got it she would flip.

Soon after that I went home and six members of her family were there. She smiled, handing me an interim barring order. According to one of the men in AMEN, this situation is quite common.

The case was heard ten days later. All I wanted was for her to go and see a psychologist to make sure she was fit to look after the children. She asked the same of me. I agreed to stay away from the house and we agreed to get psychologists' reports.

The first two months were the hardest. I started drinking. I had the kids two days a week and twenty-four hours at the weekend. Another blow was when my little girl told me my best friend had stayed in the box room!

My wife phoned and said she wanted to get back. We met with the kids in a fairground. At one stage she was very busy and animated texting and I saw the text and got the number. Later I phoned the number and it was a guy I knew indirectly through work. He wanted to see me. He had been having an affair with my wife for five months of our marriage and he was now afraid his wife was going to find out.

This finished it for me. I asked my wife not to bring a man into the house with the girls. My trust was completely eroded. I dropped the allegations and went for the separation as I wanted things to be amicable.

When I meet my wife now it is like meeting a stranger. I did ten weekly sessions with AMEN and it was the best thing I ever did. I learned about relationships and about psychology. A big part of it was about forgiveness and moving on.

Thankfully I am now able to be a support to other men who are living with domestic violence.

Marathon Woman

Frances Franklin, Cork

I was in my forties and had five small children. We had a mobile home and we were in Mornington near Drogheda at the time and suddenly one night I was coughing all night long. The next morning I went to Drogheda hospital and they said it might be asthma and sent me home.

Then one day at home I became very ill and weak. My husband was sent for at work and I went back to hospital again and it was then diagnosed that I definitely did have asthma. I was getting injections of steroids. A pattern started to emerge. I would be in and out of hospital for one to two weeks, then back home for one to two weeks, then back into hospital. It was severe. I was at death's door a couple of times and I remember once having to be helped into a doctor's surgery.

I started to attend Doctor O'Callaghan in the Bon Secours Hospital and he found a medication that suited me. Meanwhile, I had to have a hysterectomy and the surgeon was alarmed at my bone density, which was decreasing at an alarming rate. She told me I had to do weight-bearing exercise. I thought this was weight-lifting and didn't realise it was walking she meant. My son, Eoin, who was still in school, was into weights and was delighted to help his mammy. He had a bench and showed me what to do.

After eighteen months, I had another scan and the nurse asked me why I had been sent for the scan. She couldn't believe that my bone density had been so low eighteen months previously. My bone density was now as high as it possibly could be.

Around this time it was our twenty-fifth wedding anniversary and my husband bought me a treadmill. I never ran on the road but followed my son's programmes. Also at this time also we moved from Dublin to my home town of Lahinch. I was a teacher and I took early retirement. I was walking and running on the treadmill and watching the TV. One day I said to Eoin, 'Guess how far I ran today?' Thirteen miles.

He said, 'Do you know what you have to do now? You have to keep on going and run a marathon!' By this time Eoin had abandoned his degree in architecture for sports science and he gave me a training programme to follow.

Part of my training was on the treadmill but now I also went on the road. One daughter would come along with me and we'd run from Lahinch to Liscannor and then down on to the beach and into the cold water to freeze the muscles. I never had any injuries as a result of doing that. I ran the Dublin Marathon in 2001.

In our little souvenir shop in Lahinch, my husband got talking to an American with the same surname as us, Franklin. This man, Bill Franklin, turned out to be a respiratory specialist in Boston. He invited me there and did more than twenty tests on me. He said I did not have allergic asthma but what was known as clinical asthma. After I started training for the marathon there was a huge improvement in my asthma and I haven't had an attack in twelve years.

From then on I did a mix of things. Eoin was getting me to work my body. I would attend him twice a week for my programme at One-to-One Fitness in Limerick and then go back to my own gym. By then he had his own VO2 Max machine, which measures the amount of oxygen and carbon dioxide that is exchanged breath for breath. I ran the Paris Marathon in 2003, Edinburgh in 2005, London in 2006 and Cork in 2007.

I am sixty-five now. I did six or seven of the BUPA

Great North Run from Newcastle to South Shields, which is the biggest half-marathon in the world. I had a daughter living in Middlesborough and I would go over to her and she would run with me. Last year I did the Great North Run again. By now it had become a family thing. My daughter's husband began running with us too. After ten miles something happened and my leg got sore.

I am now awaiting an operation for – I suppose – a pin in my ankle. As soon as that is sorted I'll be back again. I keep my upper body going. I am still training but not running. You have to keep the heart rate up all the time. That's what helps my asthma. I still take a preventative inhaler and tablets at night. The asthma made me miserable before I started running and with five young children I probably wasn't great about taking my medication. I wasn't doing any exercise except running around the house and taking the children to things after school. I am one hundred per cent sure that starting to be active and taking up running has made a huge improvement in the quality of my life.

BONGIORNO PRINCIPESSA

Lucy, Dublin

I don't think my story is any different from a million other stories women will tell you about love, loss, finding oneself in all the mess and making something beautiful at the end.

When I was much younger, about twelve years old, I remember thinking about getting married to a man whose first wife had died and left behind two young children. I thought about it quite a few times over the years and somehow knew that was going to be me.

I had not thought about the memory too much recently but when I found the reality starting to happen the earlier memories came back to me. It just added to the rightness of it all.

I had known William for several years. We were close friends. I was coming out of a long-term relationship and turned to him for support and warmth, saying to him, 'Don't worry, I'm not going to fall in love with you.' He was summer-time after a long winter. He was warmth and relaxed fun personified. He used to call out to me in the mornings, 'Bongiorno Principessa,' a line from my favourite film, *La Vita e Bella/Life Is Beautiful*, and he had the same madcap quality as the character in the film, as well as being small and balding like him! I always roared laughing, as if hearing it each time for the first time. He had so many qualities I loved. He wrote me a poem about the end of my relationship with my ex, ringing me to read it to me. The tenderness coming through the phone line was palpable and the way he lit some fire in me was incredible. The words of his poem came dancing into my imagination and lighting my way home. I felt as if I had come out of a long darkness and he was my candle.

When our relationship started I remember feeling so alive and in tune with everything. It was as if the picture had gone from black and white to high-definition colour, the sound had come on from a silent screen. It was a beautiful, joyful and soulful beginning. I knew without question he was my soulmate.

For years my midriff had been cold, no matter what the time of year. Now, overnight, my midriff was warm. He had literally warmed the cockles of my heart!

Very early in the relationship, much to my initial

shock and dismay, I found myself pregnant. He was away in America at the time. I waited for him to return before I told him. I met him at the airport with his children and knew that I was looking at my future family.

When we got home to his house we sat in his garden and I told him our news. Not for a second did I doubt his reaction in spite of the timing being so early in our relationship, with his wife dead only a year. He told me he loved me and that he would take care of me. Very simply, with no fuss, sitting under his fruit tree, on a plastic chair, he asked me to marry him. It was simple and old-fashioned: no grand gestures, no melodrama. That afternoon, we went house-hunting and saw a dream house by the sea. We were going to have four children: his two, a daughter and son, my son and our child. We went for a walk on the beach in front of the house with the children, I remember wishing we were on our own to enjoy the time.

Throughout the next few months we had many really happy times but these were intermingled with periods of darkness and bizarre moments when William's mood-changes were hard to make sense of and seemed unconnected to the events that gave rise to them. In spite of this we got married. I loved

him with all my heart and he made me happy so I
coped with the other feelings that came up, trying
to find aspects of my own behaviour and reactions
that I could change to deal better with the situation
next time round. Eleven months after we got together
romantically our amazing, angelic daughter was
born. From the moment she came home from the
hospital I could almost see the light around her. She
drew the whole family closer, bringing us all fully into
connection for the first time. She was a part of all of
us; we were in her and she was in us. She became the
thread between us. Suddenly we had a common DNA
link.

When our daughter was eighteen months old we
got married. I woke on my wedding morning feeling
calm and brimming over with the rightness of what I
was doing. I did not have any doubts, just a feeling of
love in my heart for this man. He made me laugh; I
felt a peace with him; he got me; I loved the bones of
him. There were difficulties but I knew from a course
we had undertaken with other step-parents that we
were starting a long cycle in creating a step-parent
family, which is built upon loss from the beginning
and therefore never going to be the Waltons. I was
told afterwards that I ran up the aisle, I swung out of
the church bell when I arrived in the church grounds,

giddy with joy. My dad said later it was like a 'fairy dream': the church was full of candles and the ivy my bridesmaid and I had decorated it with the night before. The harpist played and the hymns were sung, words from John O'Donoghue's *Anam Cara* were read. I felt the simplicity of our love wrapped around the crevices of the church, bouncing back at us in the light from the candles.

Our honeymoon, in a little cottage in Andalucia, looking out on to a mountain of olives every morning through an old oak window, gave us a view into a world that was fertile and barren at the same time. We had a week in the land of olives, goats, tapas, port, vino and dry mountains and it was our paradise. While we were making love one day on a fertile hillside, the echo of olives being beaten off the tree rippling across to us from the opposite hillside, William was stung on his backside by a bee. It represented the fullness of life and made us both laugh.

Our return home was with a crash. We were thrown rudely back into reality to our four children, work, domestic routine. William's mother had just had a stroke. From that point the slide downhill was sudden. I was wearing no seat belt to prepare me for the crash.

No details of what occurred are necessary: it is

enough to say the following months brought me to the edge of myself, into dark places I will never go again. My mental health and wellbeing were severely tested; my sense of me disappeared piece by piece. I remember one dark night cycling from the station on my return from work, on a dark country road with no lighting, and turning off my bike lamp just to be in the darkness. I felt alive again. I was being reckless and loved it.

Eighteen months after our wedding I roared out from my belly, 'This marriage is over!' An incident from which there was no return left me with no choice. There are some things women know from the depths of our souls, truths that rise up, that cannot be kept down, no matter how much our shadow side wants to cling desperately to what we have. I recall looking at his shoes on the floor and seeing all his goodness in his shoes. I wanted the man who was like his shoes, not the other part that was in darkness.

After William left the house I spent the following three years untangling the pieces of my story that had led me to this place. I spent many nights crying and howling, releasing a deep sorrow from my soul, a broken dream where another dream has now been created. My story of hope is the person I have become. William was my soulmate because of the painful lessons I needed to learn in this lifetime, lessons I learned because of him. I was a child sleep-walking and now I am a wisdom-keeper, the keeper of who I am. I know I need no one else to make me happy or complete me; I do that for myself now. Now I see people's energy for what it is, so I can be discerning about where and when and with whom I immerse myself in relationships. I enjoy being single and have never felt so loved and actually 'unsingle'. There is a fullness in being single which is not celebrated enough, pleasures in my own company that are beyond words. I have been on a spiritual journey for the past three years, which started in India, the land of high vibrations and home of my ancestors, after my separation.

My story of hope is echoed by many women all around the world. Like the snake we shed many skins. It is a part of our evolution to journey forward, our souls calling us to fulfil our potential by listening to that call, our collective story of hope becoming a beautiful patchwork. Whether we journey alone or with another, listening to the authentic voice of our souls is the greatest gift we can give to ourselves and to the world.